CRITICAL THINKING ACTIVITIES

IN
PATTERNS,
IMAGERY,
LOGIC

Dale Seymour   Ed Beardslee

DALE SEYMOUR PUBLICATIONS

Cover design by Rachel Gage

DS01908
ISBN 0-86651-472-4

DALE
SEYMOUR
PUBLICATIONS
P.O. BOX 10888
PALO ALTO, CA 94303

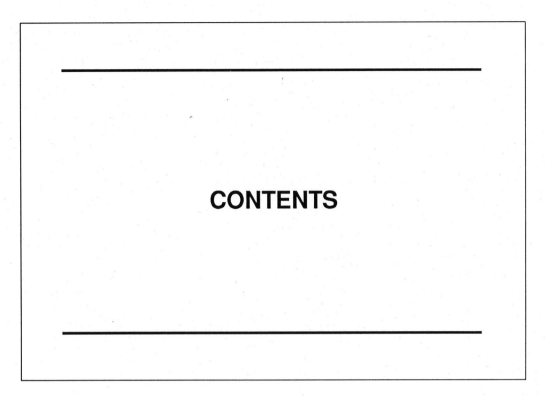

CONTENTS

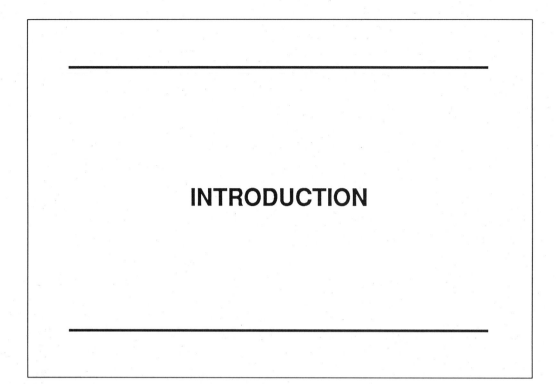

INTRODUCTION

Thinking skills and problem solving are currently given high priority in curriculum development and inservice programs. Although each area of the curriculum defines and approaches thinking skills and problem solving somewhat differently, the basic emphasis on teaching students how to think and how to learn has strong support from most people concerned with the education of youngsters.

Too often, thinking skills have been overlooked or considered extra, something above and beyond the basics that must be taught. Teachers need to recognize that thinking skills *are* basic. The term *critical thinking skills* is a good one because the word *critical* has a number of different meanings. It means *analytical,* and it means *evaluative* or *judgmental,* but it also means *indispensable, vital, essential.* Indeed, critical thinking activities should be considered indispensable to the education of every child.

This book presents activities to help students develop their thinking and problem-solving skills. Mathematics curriculum specialists have identified from ten to fifteen strategies that can help students solve nonroutine math problems. Often students may need to use more than one such strategy to arrive at the solution for a given problem. Some of these strategies require that students use skills such as thinking visually, recognizing patterns, using logical reasoning, and doing organized counting—all of which are elements of critical thinking in mathematics.

There are a number of different ways to categorize thinking skills. No two authors would choose the same list or prioritize the importance of each skill in the same way. This book concentrates on three specific types of thinking skills: *patterns, imagery,* and *logic.* If students are to become successful problem solvers, they need to become good critical thinkers at the same time.

How to Use This Book

As a supplement to a regular textbook this book provides materials that can be used in a variety of ways to introduce, reinforce, and elaborate on specific critical thinking skills.

Reproducible Pages

The pages in this book are designed to be photocopied for distribution to students as individual worksheets or problem cards. Preparing a transparency of any page (using a photocopy machine and transparency acetate) makes it possible to present a lesson to a group or to the entire class by using an overhead projector.

Sequence

In general, there is no recommended sequence for presenting the topics or the activities within a single topic. Teachers may choose and order the activities in whatever way they believe will best meet their instructional goals. Activities within a topic are generally ordered from simpler to more difficult, as indicated by their one-diamond, two-diamond, or three-diamond rating.

Class Discussion

Students develop their thinking skills by observing how other people think. For this reason, class discussion of the activities for every topic is invaluable. Teachers are advised to spend class time discussing different ways to formulate problems and brainstorming possible approaches to their solution. Students need help in overcoming the misconception that in math there is always one exact answer and only one way to solve the problem. Teachers need to encourage and reward creativity and divergent thinking in these activities.

Teaching Suggestions by Topic

Part 1: Patterns

Mathematics is often defined as the *study of patterns.* Making students conscious of patterns can help them to see important relationships in mathematics. Number patterns are a nonthreatening way to help students learn about special number properties. Students should be encouraged to create their own patterns—both visual and numerical.

Organized counting dovetails nicely with pattern recognition. A student soon learns that multiplication is a shortcut to counting or adding. Breaking a problem into smaller parts may be easier than approaching it as a whole. Students should talk about the advantages and disadvantages of approaching a problem through the organized counting of patterns.

For exercises in which students are asked to continue a given pattern, there may be more than one solution. Teachers should not be too quick to assume that a student's answer is wrong just because it is different; examining that pattern may show that the student has discovered a perfectly good pattern of his or her own.

Part 2: Imagery

The ability to visualize is extremely helpful in solving problems. In the regular curriculum, students rarely have an opportunity to develop visual-thinking skills. In addition to providing much-needed practice, these lessons may serve as models for teachers who wish to create similar activities for further work in imagery and visual thinking.

Many of the activities in this section lend themselves to elaboration. Students should be encouraged to look for geometric shapes and visual patterns in their environment. They might bring in clippings from magazines and newspapers to illustrate such concepts as symmetry, congruence, rotation, and similarity. Most students enjoy creating their own designs that allow them to explore geometric relationships.

Part 3: Logic

For many students, the worksheets on logic will be more difficult than others in this book. Consequently, teachers are advised to take the additional time needed to explain the conventions of Venn diagrams and to provide model solutions. Students should be shown how to formulate their own questions, for this can enhance their understanding of the principles and structure of logic problems. Logic problems that seem overwhelmingly complex can often be simplified by breaking the problem into smaller problems. Students who do this will discover that taking one small step at a time can lead them to a solution.

You may need to give special attention to the terminology of Venn diagrams. Some students may be especially confused by the terms *both, and, either, or,* and *only.* For example, *in A and B* means "within the sections where A and B meet"; *either* means "in A or in B or in the section where A and B meet"; *in A only* means "in the portion of A that is not shared by any other shape." Examples are given in the text to clarify these terms.

Making Successful Thinkers and Problem Solvers

Students will see themselves as good problem solvers if they experience repeated success. Thus, when first introducing new critical thinking activities in any topic, it is better to err in selecting pages that are too easy than to have students struggle and conclude that they are unable to solve nonroutine problems. Through class discussion and work within small groups, students will have the chance to observe the thinking strategies of their peers. Eventually, they will muster the confidence to explore possible solution strategies on their own. At this point, they will be well on their way to becoming proficient critical thinkers in all their mathematics work.

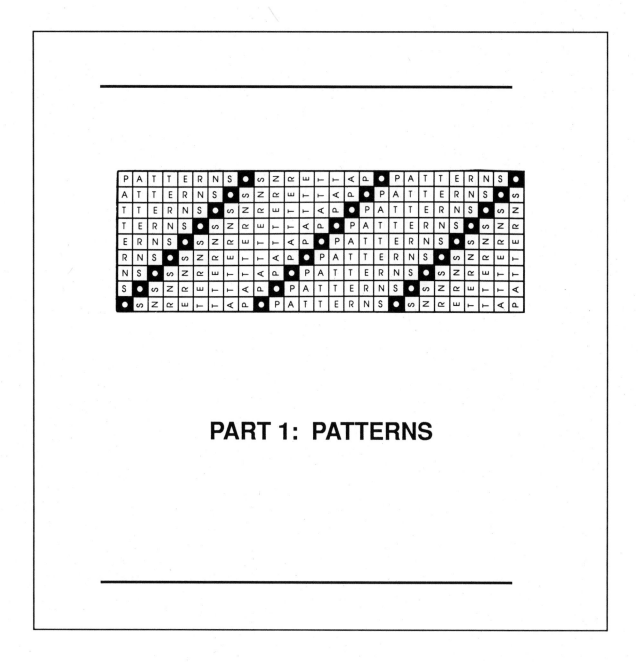

PART 1: PATTERNS

REVERSALS

Experiment with this three-step procedure. An interesting pattern results!

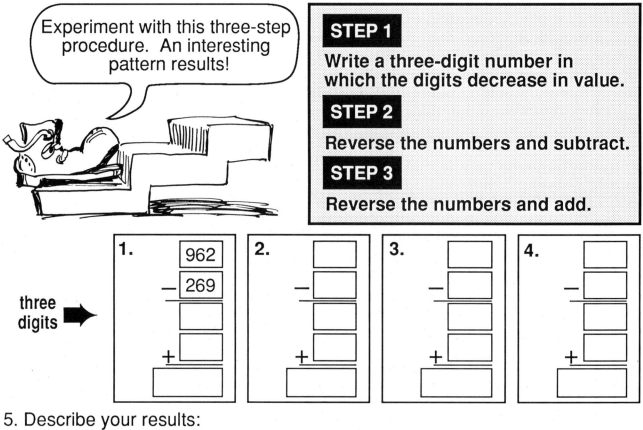

STEP 1
Write a three-digit number in which the digits decrease in value.

STEP 2
Reverse the numbers and subtract.

STEP 3
Reverse the numbers and add.

three digits ➡

1.
962
− 269

2.
−
+

3.
−
+

4.
−
+

5. Describe your results:

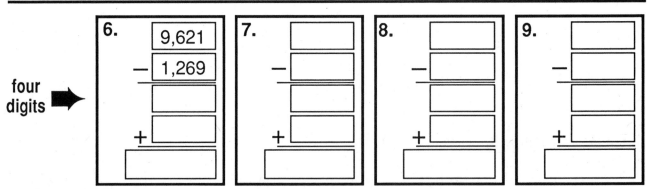

four digits ➡

6.
9,621
− 1,269

7.
−
+

8.
−
+

9.
−
+

10. Describe your results:

11. Can you predict the results of this experiment with a five-digit number in which the digits decrease in value? Try some examples to check your guess.

12. Try predicting the results with six-, seven-, and eight-digit numbers. Use a calculator to check out your guesses.

CRITICAL THINKING ACTIVITIES IN PATTERNS, IMAGERY, LOGIC (Secondary)

PATTERNS OF MULTIPLES AND FACTORS (I) ◆

Two is a *factor* of six, since 2 × 3 = 6.

Six is a *multiple* of two, since 6 ÷ 2 = 3.

1. Fill in the blanks to give consecutive multiples of 2.

    2, 4, 6, 8, 10, 12, _____, 16, _____, 20, 22, _____, _____, 28, 30, _____,

    _____, _____, _____, _____.

2. All the multiples of 2 are even numbers. All even numbers
    are multiples of _____.

3. Even numbers end in _____, _____, _____, _____, or _____.

4. Multiples of 2 end in _____, _____, _____, _____, or _____.

5. Draw a ring around each number that is a multiple of 2.

    a. 46   b. 108   c. 37   d. 900   e. 1,001   f. 2,342   g. 4,416

    h. 1,354   i. 8,883   j. 49   k. 57,206   l. 57,207   m. 115,804,216

6. Draw a ring around each even number.

    a. 66   b. 84   c. 100   d. 35   e. 111   f. 404   g. 309   h. 202

    i. 983   j. 33,204   k. 33,205   l. 517,336

7. Draw a ring around each number that has 2 as a factor.

    a. 88   b. 62   c. 57   d. 40   e. 76   f. 204   g. 115   h. 328

    i. 241   j. 2,143   k. 2,144   l. 83,998

8. True or false: If the last digit of a number is divisible by 2,
    that number is divisible by 2. _____

9. Draw a ring around each number that has 2 as a factor.

    a. 111,334   b. 808,465   c. 135,796   d. 1,323,458   e. 263,842,903

    f. 10,000,000,000   g. 1,234,567,890,123   h. 987,654,321,098

    i. 8 million   j. four million, seven hundred twenty-three thousand, five

PATTERNS OF MULTIPLES AND FACTORS (II) ◆

Multiples of 10 are numbers that are divisible by 10 without remainders.

1. Fill in the missing multiples of 10.

   10, 20, 30, ____, 50, ____, ____, 80, ____, ____, 110, 120, ____,

   ____, _____, 160, ____, ____, _____

2. All the multiples of 10 above end in ____.

3. If a number ends in 0, we can say the number is a

   _____ of 10.

4. Draw a ring around each number that is a multiple of 10.

   a. 480   b. 604   c. 1,000   d. 1,005   e. 84,360   f. 215,000

   g. 78,650   h. 835,778

5. Fill in the missing multiples of 5.

   a. 5, 10, 15, 20, ____, 30, ____, 40, ____, ____, 55

   b. 135, 140, ____, 150, ____, _____, ____, ____

6. All multiples of 5 end in _____ or _____.

7. Draw a ring around each number that is a multiple of 5.

   a. 13   b. 204   c. 335   d. 1,000   e. 7,554   f. 15,375   g. 98,430

   h. 555,565   i. 123,456,789,000   j. 500,000,406

8. If a number ends in 0 or 5, it is divisible by _____.

9. If a number ends in 0, it is divisible by _____.

10. Fill in the missing multiples of 3.

    a. 3, 6, 9, ____, 15, 18, ____, ____, ____, 30
    b. 111, 114, ____, 120, ____, _____, ____, 132

Each multiple of 3 has digits whose sum is divisible by 3.
Example: $12 \rightarrow 2 + 1 = 3$ $15 \rightarrow 1 + 5 = 6$ $18 \rightarrow 1 + 8 = 9$

11. Draw a ring around each number that is divisible by 3.

    a. 112   b. 501   c. 1,113   d. 2,226   e. 300,111

12. Each number whose digits total a multiple of 3 is _____.

CRITICAL THINKING ACTIVITIES IN PATTERNS, IMAGERY, LOGIC (Secondary)
© Dale Seymour Publications

PATTERNS OF DIVISIBILITY

A number is divisible by 2 if it ends in 0, 2, 4, 6, or 8.
A number is divisible by 3 if the sum of its digits is divisible by 3.

1. Draw a ring around each number that is divisible by 2.

    a. 157,206   b. 3,498,551   c. 77,086,540

2. Draw a ring around each number that is divisible by 3.

    a. 20,100   b. 42,001   c. 1,200,500

A number is divisible by 6 if it is divisible by both 2 and 3. That means the number must be even (ending in 0, 2, 4, 6, or 8) *and* the sum of its digits must be divisible by 3.

3. Draw a ring around each number that is divisible by 6.

    a. 33,000   b. 11,031   c. 20,000   d. 33,333

    e. 12,306   f. 12,309   g. 30,021   h. 30,012

A number is divisible by 9 if the sum of its digits is divisible by 9. *Example:* 9 → 9 18 → 1 + 8 = 9 27 → 2 + 7 = 9

4. Draw a ring around each number that is divisible by 9.

    a. 333   b. 30,033   c. 40,033   d. 111,000   e. 99,981

    f. 99,918   g. 99,927   h. 90,936   i. 504,000   j. 405,000

    k. 500,400   l. 500,004   m. 123,456   n. 123,456,780   o. 111,111,101

    p. 901,800,000   q. 200,500,100,100   r. 810,018,270,360,000

5. Make a check in the chart if the number is divisible by 2, 3, 6, or 9.

Number	÷ by 2	÷ by 3	÷ by 6	÷ by 9
9		✔		✔
12				
15				
20				
39				
66				

VISUAL PATTERNS (I)

Continue each pattern.

1.

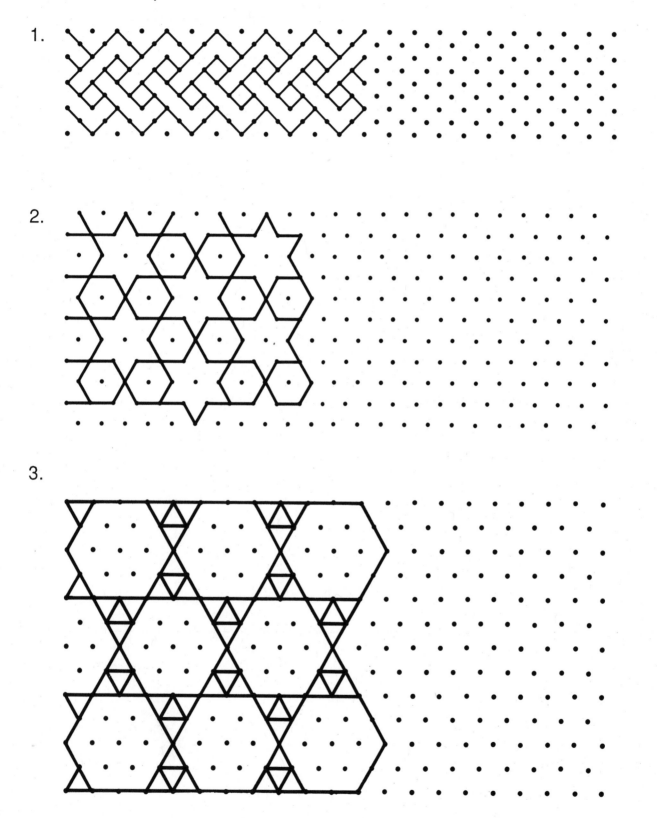

2.

3.

CRITICAL THINKING ACTIVITIES IN PATTERNS, IMAGERY, LOGIC (Secondary)
© Dale Seymour Publications

LOGIC PATTERNS (I)

◆

1. Write at least one number in each of the seven sections.

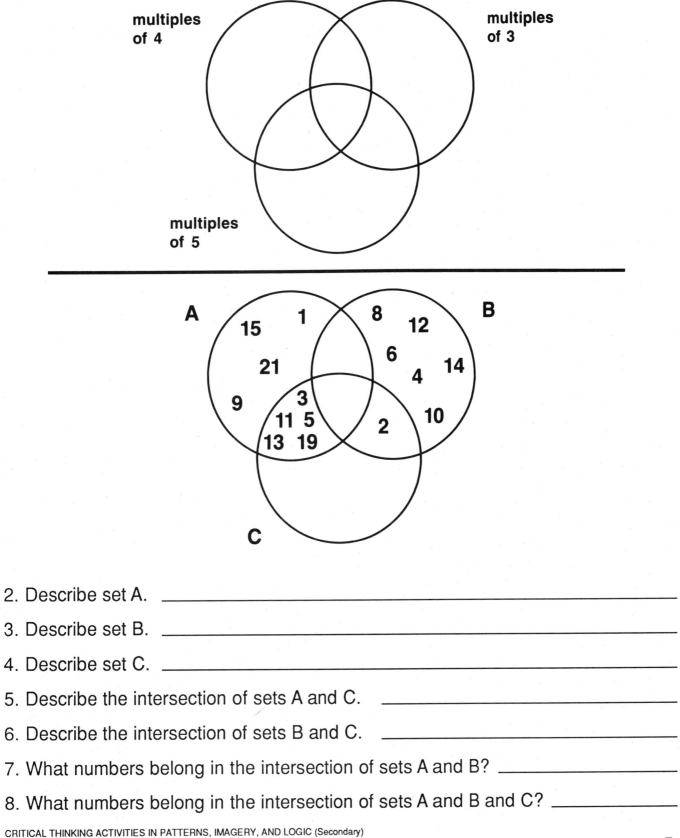

2. Describe set A. _____

3. Describe set B. _____

4. Describe set C. _____

5. Describe the intersection of sets A and C. _____

6. Describe the intersection of sets B and C. _____

7. What numbers belong in the intersection of sets A and B? _____

8. What numbers belong in the intersection of sets A and B and C? _____

DIGIT-SUM AVERAGE

Which numbers have digit-sum averages that are whole numbers?

		Digit-Sum Average	**Is it a whole number?**	
Examples:	258	$\dfrac{2 + 5 + 8}{3} = \dfrac{15}{3} = 5$	(Yes)	No
	53	$\dfrac{5 + 3}{2} = \dfrac{8}{2} = 4$	(Yes)	No
	61	$\dfrac{6 + 1}{2} = \dfrac{7}{2} = 3\dfrac{1}{2}$	Yes	(No)
1.	76	_____	Yes	No
2.	84	_____	Yes	No
3.	25	_____	Yes	No
4.	37	_____	Yes	No
5.	91	_____	Yes	No
6.	151	_____	Yes	No
7.	204	_____	Yes	No
8.	963	_____	Yes	No
9.	512	_____	Yes	No
10.	780	_____	Yes	No

11. Examine the two-digit numbers. Propose a rule that produces a whole number:

_____

12. Examine the three-digit numbers. Propose a rule that produces a whole number:

_____

CRITICAL THINKING ACTIVITIES IN PATTERNS, IMAGERY, LOGIC (Secondary)
© Dale Seymour Publications

MATCH THE RULE (I)

◆

1. Draw a ring around all of the equations that do *not* match this general equation: $\dfrac{1}{M} + \dfrac{1}{M} = \dfrac{2}{M}$

A. $\dfrac{1}{3} + \dfrac{1}{4} = \dfrac{7}{12}$

B. $\dfrac{1}{3} + \dfrac{1}{3} = \dfrac{2}{3}$

C. $\dfrac{1}{2} + \dfrac{1}{4} = \dfrac{3}{4}$

D. $\dfrac{1}{967} + \dfrac{1}{967} = \dfrac{2}{967}$

E. $\dfrac{1}{8} + \dfrac{1}{4} = \dfrac{3}{8}$

F. $\dfrac{1}{5} + \dfrac{1}{5} = \dfrac{2}{5}$

G. $\dfrac{1}{19} + \dfrac{1}{19} = \dfrac{2}{19}$

H. $\dfrac{1}{3.5} + \dfrac{1}{3.5} = \dfrac{2}{3.5}$

Why don't the equations match?

_____

2. Draw a ring around all of the equations that do *not* match this general equation: $\dfrac{1}{M} + \dfrac{N}{M} = \dfrac{1+N}{M}$

A. $\dfrac{1}{3} + \dfrac{1}{3} = \dfrac{1+1}{3}$

B. $\dfrac{2}{3} + \dfrac{1}{3} = \dfrac{2+1}{3}$

C. $\dfrac{1}{8} + \dfrac{5}{8} = \dfrac{1+5}{8}$

D. $\dfrac{3}{11} + \dfrac{4}{11} = \dfrac{3+4}{11}$

E. $\dfrac{1}{15} + \dfrac{27}{15} = \dfrac{1+27}{15}$

F. $\dfrac{1}{23} + \dfrac{9}{23} = \dfrac{1+9}{23}$

G. $\dfrac{2}{9} + \dfrac{8}{9} = \dfrac{2+8}{9}$

H. $\dfrac{1}{1} + \dfrac{3}{1} = \dfrac{1+3}{1}$

Why don't the equations match?

_____

3. Draw a ring around all of the equations that do *not* match this general equation: $\dfrac{P}{M} + \dfrac{N}{M} = \dfrac{P+N}{M}$

A. $\dfrac{1}{3} + \dfrac{2}{3} = \dfrac{1+2}{3}$

B. $\dfrac{3}{7} + \dfrac{4}{7} = \dfrac{3+4}{7}$

C. $\dfrac{2}{8} + \dfrac{1}{4} = \dfrac{2+2}{8}$

D. $\dfrac{1}{3} + \dfrac{1}{4} = \dfrac{3+4}{12}$

E. $\dfrac{7}{15} + \dfrac{2}{15} = \dfrac{7+2}{15}$

F. $\dfrac{1}{12} + \dfrac{1}{6} = \dfrac{1+2}{12}$

G. $\dfrac{1}{7} + \dfrac{1}{8} = \dfrac{8+7}{56}$

H. $\dfrac{9}{23} + \dfrac{2}{23} = \dfrac{9+2}{23}$

Why don't the equations match?

MATCH THE RULE (II)

◆

1. Draw a ring around all of the equations that are similar:

A. $\dfrac{1}{2} + \dfrac{2}{2} = \dfrac{3}{2}$ B. $\dfrac{1}{5} + \dfrac{2}{5} = \dfrac{3}{5}$ C. $\dfrac{1}{7} + \dfrac{2}{7} = \dfrac{3}{7}$

D. $\dfrac{1}{6} + \dfrac{2}{6} = \dfrac{1}{2}$ E. $\dfrac{1}{2} + \dfrac{2}{3} = \dfrac{7}{6}$ F. $\dfrac{1}{9} + \dfrac{2}{9} = \dfrac{3}{9}$

G. $\dfrac{1}{29} + \dfrac{2}{29} = \dfrac{3}{29}$ H. $\dfrac{1}{1.6} + \dfrac{2}{1.6} = \dfrac{3}{1.6}$

Write the general equation for these similar equations:

---

2. Draw a ring around all of the equations that are similar:

A. $\dfrac{4}{7} + \dfrac{3}{7} = \dfrac{4+3}{7}$ B. $\dfrac{2}{5} + \dfrac{1}{5} = \dfrac{2+1}{5}$ C. $\dfrac{2}{3} + \dfrac{0}{3} = \dfrac{2+0}{3}$

D. $\dfrac{2}{9} + \dfrac{3}{9} = \dfrac{2+3}{9}$ E. $\dfrac{2}{11} + \dfrac{5}{11} = \dfrac{2+5}{11}$ F. $\dfrac{2}{13} + \dfrac{4}{13} = \dfrac{2+4}{13}$

G. $\dfrac{2}{27} + \dfrac{9}{27} = \dfrac{2+9}{27}$ H. $\dfrac{3}{15} + \dfrac{4}{15} = \dfrac{3+4}{15}$

Write the general equation for these similar equations:

CRITICAL THINKING ACTIVITIES IN PATTERNS, IMAGERY, LOGIC (Secondary)
© Dale Seymour Publications

KAPREKAR'S CONSTANT

The number 6,174 is called Kaprekar's Constant. It was named
after the Russian mathematician who discovered this result in 1955.

Example:

Start with any four-digit number. (All digits may not be the same.)   2,916

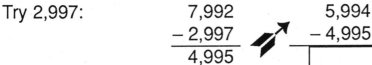

$$
\begin{array}{r}
\text{Order the digits high to low.} \quad 9,621 \\
\text{Then order them low to high and subtract.} \quad -1,269 \\
\hline
8,352
\end{array}
$$

Repeat the process: High to low   8,532
Low to high $-2,358$
Difference $\overline{6,174}$

What did you observe? _____

Try 1998:

	High to low			
High to low	9,981		8,820		8,532
Low to high	−1,899		− 288		− 2,358
Difference	8,082		8,532		☐

Try 7344:

High to low	7,443		☐	☐	☐
Low to high	−3,447		− ☐	− ☐	− ☐
Difference	3,996		☐	☐	☐

Try a four-digit number of your own.
Describe the results: _____

Try this variation using the number 3,142:
Reorder only the first and last digits   3,142
keeping the middle two the same: − 2,143
Subtract: ☐

Try 2,997:

	7,992		5,994
	− 2,997		− 4,995
	4,995		☐

Try another four-digit number. Describe your results: _____

NUMBER PATTERNS (I)

Look at the numbers in each box. What do the numbers have in common?

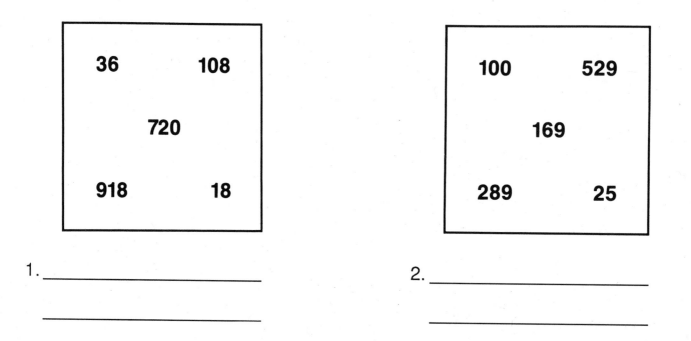

1. _____

   _____

2. _____

   _____

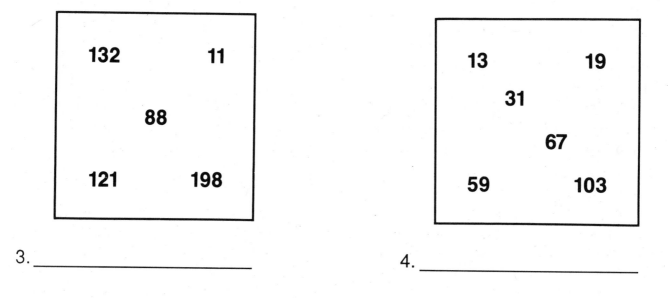

3. _____

   _____

4. _____

   _____

CRITICAL THINKING ACTIVITIES IN PATTERNS, IMAGERY, LOGIC (Secondary)
© Dale Seymour Publications

HUNDREDS CHART PATTERNS (I)

◆

0	1	2	3	4	5	6	7	8	9
10	11	12	13	14	15	16	17	18	19
20	21	22	23	24	25	26	27	28	29
30	31	32	33	34	35	36	37	38	39
40	41	42	43	44	45	46	47	48	49
50	51	52	53	54	55	56	57	58	59
60	61	62	63	64	65	66	67	68	69
70	71	72	73	74	75	76	77	78	79
80	81	82	83	84	85	86	87	88	89
90	91	92	93	94	95	96	97	98	99

Mentally place the box-and-circle figure on the chart so that a number is in each box and circle. Add the numbers in the four boxes and record their sum. Multiply the number in the center circle by 4 and record the answer. What do you notice?

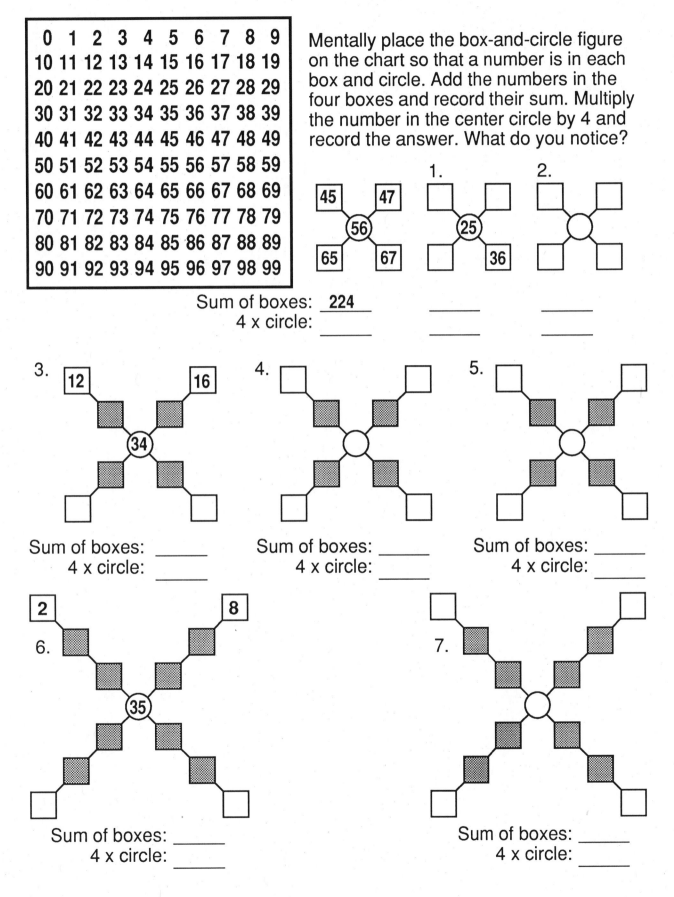

Sum of boxes: __224__   _____   _____
4 x circle: _____   _____   _____

Sum of boxes: _____
4 x circle: _____

Sum of boxes: _____
4 x circle: _____

Sum of boxes: _____
4 x circle: _____

Sum of boxes: _____
4 x circle: _____

Sum of boxes: _____
4 x circle: _____

ADDITION TABLE PATTERNS (I) ◆

+	0	1	2	3	4	5	6	7	8	9
0	0	1	2	3	4	5	6	7	8	9
1	1	2	3	4	5	6	7	8	9	10
2	2	3	4	5	6	7	8	9	10	11
3	3	4	5	6	7	8	9	10	11	12
4	4	5	6	7	8	9	10	11	12	13
5	5	6	7	8	9	10	11	12	13	14
6	6	7	8	9	10	11	12	13	14	15
7	7	8	9	10	11	12	13	14	15	16
8	8	9	10	11	12	13	14	15	16	17
9	9	10	11	12	13	14	15	16	17	18

Mentally place the box-and-circle figure on the chart so that a number is in each box and circle. Add the numbers in the four boxes and record their sum. Multiply the number in the center circle by 4 and record your answer. What do you notice?

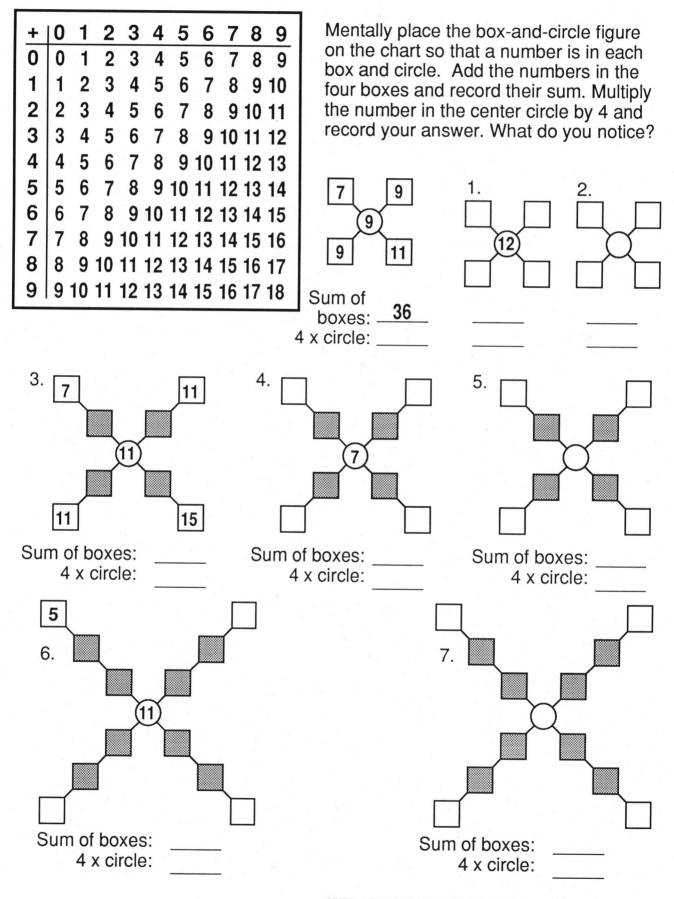

Sum of boxes: __36__
4 x circle: _____

3.
Sum of boxes: _____
4 x circle: _____

4.
Sum of boxes: _____
4 x circle: _____

5.
Sum of boxes: _____
4 x circle: _____

6.
Sum of boxes: _____
4 x circle: _____

7.
Sum of boxes: _____
4 x circle: _____

CRITICAL THINKING ACTIVITIES IN PATTERNS, IMAGERY, LOGIC (Secondary)
© Dale Seymour Publications

MULTIPLICATION TABLE PATTERNS (I) ◆

×	0	1	2	3	4	5	6	7	8	9
0	0	0	0	0	0	0	0	0	0	0
1	0	1	2	3	4	5	6	7	8	9
2	0	2	4	6	8	10	12	14	16	18
3	0	3	6	9	12	15	18	21	24	27
4	0	4	8	12	16	20	24	28	32	36
5	0	5	10	15	20	25	30	35	40	45
6	0	6	12	18	24	30	36	42	48	54
7	0	7	14	21	28	35	42	49	56	63
8	0	8	16	24	32	40	48	56	64	72
9	0	9	18	27	36	45	54	63	72	81

Mentally place the box-and-circle figure on the chart so that a number is in each box and circle. Add the numbers in the four boxes and record their sum. Multiply the number in the center circle by 4 and record your answer. What do you notice?

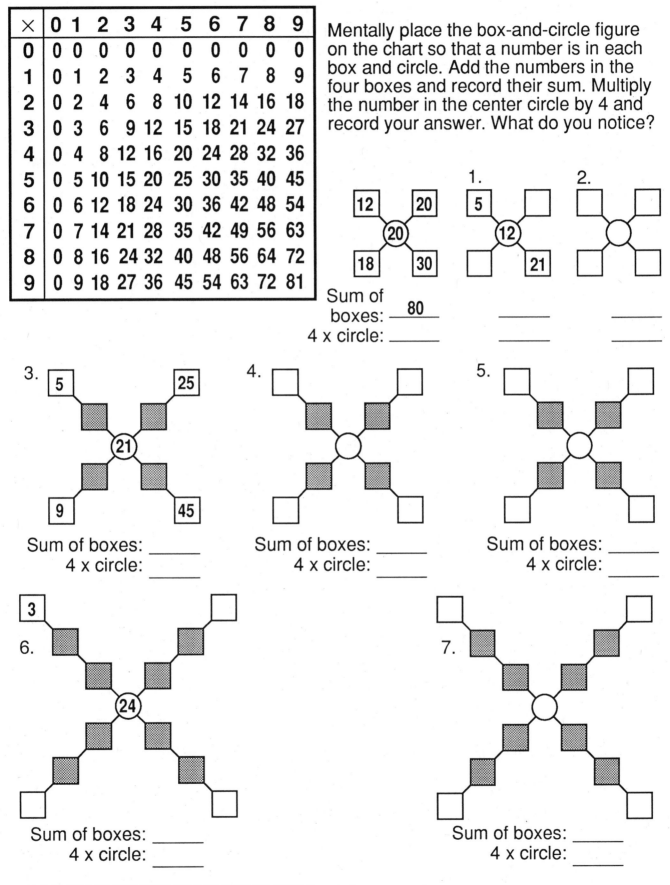

12 20
20
18 30

Sum of boxes: ___80___
4 x circle: _____

1.
5
12
21

Sum of boxes: _____
4 x circle: _____

2.

Sum of boxes: _____
4 x circle: _____

3.
5   25
21
9   45

Sum of boxes: _____
4 x circle: _____

4.

Sum of boxes: _____
4 x circle: _____

5.

Sum of boxes: _____
4 x circle: _____

6.
3
24

Sum of boxes: _____
4 x circle: _____

7.

Sum of boxes: _____
4 x circle: _____

CIRCLE PATTERNS

What You Need: a tape measure and 10 different circular objects, such as a wastebasket, a plate, a circular clock face, or a lamp shade.

What You Do: Measure the circumference (C) and diameter (D) of each object. Record the measurements in the C and D columns of the chart. Complete the chart by computing the sum, difference, product, and quotient of C and D.

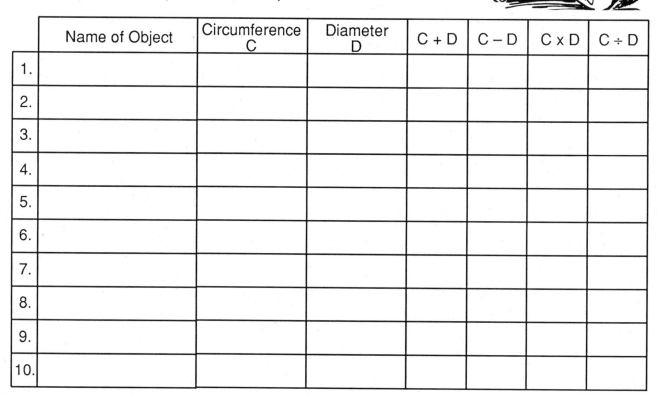

	Name of Object	Circumference C	Diameter D	C + D	C − D	C x D	C ÷ D
1.							
2.							
3.							
4.							
5.							
6.							
7.							
8.							
9.							
10.							

Examine each column to see if there is a pattern. Describe any patterns that you find:

Do you think these patterns exist with all circular objects? Explain.

CRITICAL THINKING ACTIVITIES IN PATTERNS, IMAGERY, LOGIC (Secondary)
© Dale Seymour Publications

SHADOW NUMBERS

◆

Complete each column below. Start with your own number
in the last column.

Three-digit number	826	471	380	_____
Repeat number	826,826	471,471	380,380	_____
Divide by 13	_____	_____	_____	_____
Divide by 11	_____	_____	_____	_____
Divide by 7	_____	_____	_____	_____

What number would you multiply 826 by to get 826,826?

Four-digit number	3,125	4,605	3,128	_____
Repeat number	31,253,125	46,054,605	31,283,128	_____
Divide by 73	_____	_____	_____	_____
Divide by 137	_____	_____	_____	_____

What number would you multiply 3,125 by to get 31,253,125?

What is the product of 73 and 137?

Two-digit number	23	47	19	_____
Repeat twice	232,323	474,747	191,919	_____
Divide by 3	_____	_____	_____	_____
Divide by 7	_____	_____	_____	_____
Divide by 13	_____	_____	_____	_____
Divide by 37	_____	_____	_____	_____

Explain why you get these repeating patterns:

What is a shadow number?

Come up with at least one shadow number of your own:

SUM PATTERNS

◆

Karl Friedrich Gauss was a famous mathematician. It is said that when he was 10 years old his teacher gave the class an assignment. The students were asked to find the sum of the first 100 counting numbers. Karl thought of a shortcut that allowed him to find the answer in less than a minute. Can you figure out how he did it? If not, read on.

$1 + 2 + 3 + ... + 99 + 100$

Here is a series of numbers, a set of numbers added in a patterned sequence. Each number is called a *term*.

$1 + 2 + 3 + 4 + 5 + 6 + 7 + 8 + 9 + 10$

The bracketed numbers are a pair.
A shortcut to writing the series is: $1 + 2 + \cdots + 9 + 10$.

1. What is the sum of the first and last numbers in the series above? _____

2. What is the sum of the second and ninth terms? _____

3. How many pairs of numbers are there? _____

4. The number of pairs × the sum of each pair = the sum of the series. What is the sum of this series? _____

5. How many pairs are in 100 numbers? _____

6. What is the sum of each pair? _____

7. What is the product of the number of pairs and the sum of each pair? Write the equation. _____

8. Find the sum of the first 50 counting numbers. Write the equation.

_____

9. Find $1 + 2 + 3 + \cdots + 68 + 69 + 70$. Write the equation.

_____

10. Find $1 + 2 + 3 + \cdots + 498 + 499 + 500$. Write the equation.

_____

11. From the patterns you have seen, find a rule or formula for the sum of
    $1 + 2 + 3 + \cdots + (n - 2) + (n - 1) + n$. _____

CRITICAL THINKING ACTIVITIES IN PATTERNS, IMAGERY, LOGIC (Secondary)

VISUAL PATTERNS (II)

Continue each pattern.

1.

2.

3.

LOGIC PATTERNS (II)

1. Write at least one number in each of the seven sections.

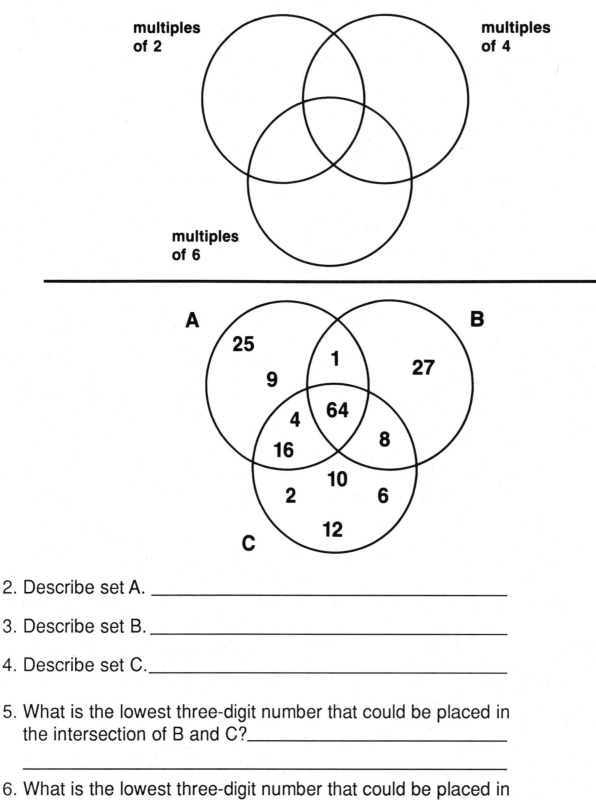

2. Describe set A. _____

3. Describe set B. _____

4. Describe set C. _____

5. What is the lowest three-digit number that could be placed in the intersection of B and C? _____
_____

6. What is the lowest three-digit number that could be placed in the intersection of A and B? _____
_____

CRITICAL THINKING ACTIVITIES IN PATTERNS, IMAGERY, LOGIC (Secondary)
© Dale Seymour Publications

NUMBER PATTERNS WITH A RULE

Each number pattern below has a rule. Study the chart, especially problem 1. Then fill in the missing numbers and rule.

	first term $n = 1$	second term $n = 2$	third term $n = 3$	fourth term $n = 4$	fifth term $n = 5$		rule for nth term	rule for $(n+1)$th term
1.	2	4	6	8	10	$\cdots$	$2n$	$2(n+1)$
2.	1	3	5	___	___	$\cdots$	$2n-1$	_____
3.	4	5	6	___	___	$\cdots$	___	$(n+1)+3$
4.	3	___	___	___	___	$\cdots$	$2n+1$	$2(n+1)+1$
5.	2	5	8	11	___	$\cdots$	___	$3(n+1)-1$
6.	5	7	9	11	___	$\cdots$	___	_____
7.	1	4	9	16	___	$\cdots$	___	$(n+1)^2$
8.	0	3	8	___	___	$\cdots$	n^2-1	_____
9.	2	8	18	___	___	$\cdots$	$2n^2$	_____
10.	4	7	___	___		$\cdots$	n^2+3	_____
11.	1	___	___	___	___	$\cdots$	n^3	_____
12.	___	___	___	___	___	$\cdots$	___	$2(n+1)^2-1$

PASCAL'S TRIANGLE (I)

◆◆

Pascal's Triangle, shown at the right, is an infinite array of numbers. The questions below are about some of the many patterns in the triangle.

← Row 0
← Row 1
← Row 2
← Row 3
← Row 4

1 4 6 4 1

Fourth row in Pascal's Triangle ⬆

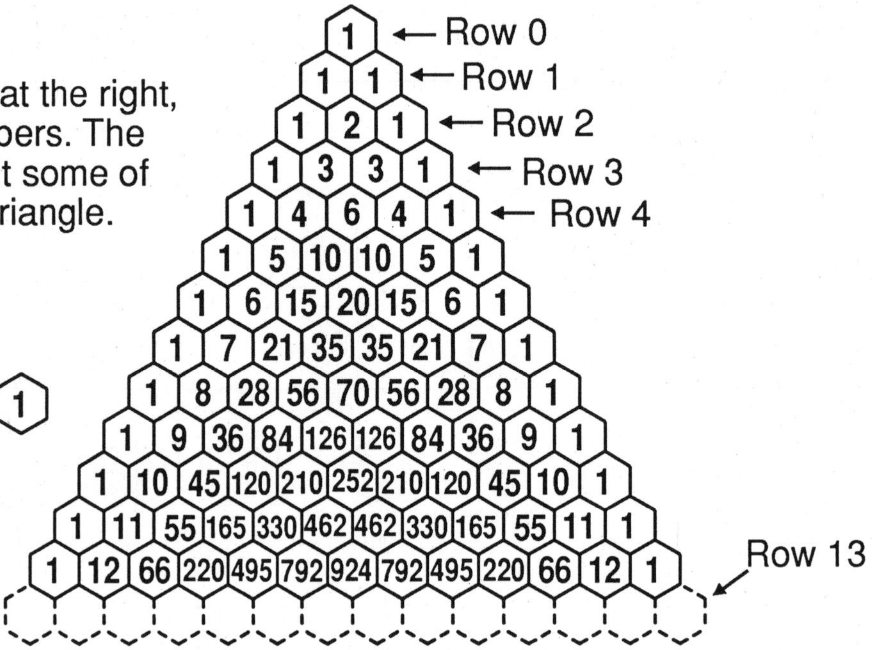

Row 13

---

1. Describe how the triangle is generated:

2. What are the two middle numbers in the 13th row?

---

3. Write the sum of each row in the blanks below:

___ ___ ___ ___ ___ ___ ___ ___ ___ ___ . . .

Describe the pattern:

---

4. Write the sum of the numbers in the 6th row as a one-digit number with an exponent.

5. Write the sum of the numbers in the 10th row as a one-digit number with an exponent.

6. Use a pattern to help find the sum of all the numbers in the 100th row.

CRITICAL THINKING ACTIVITIES IN PATTERNS, IMAGERY, LOGIC (Secondary)

PASCAL'S TRIANGLE (II)

◆◆

Pascal's Triangle, shown at the right, is an infinite array of numbers. The questions below are about some of the many patterns in the triangle.

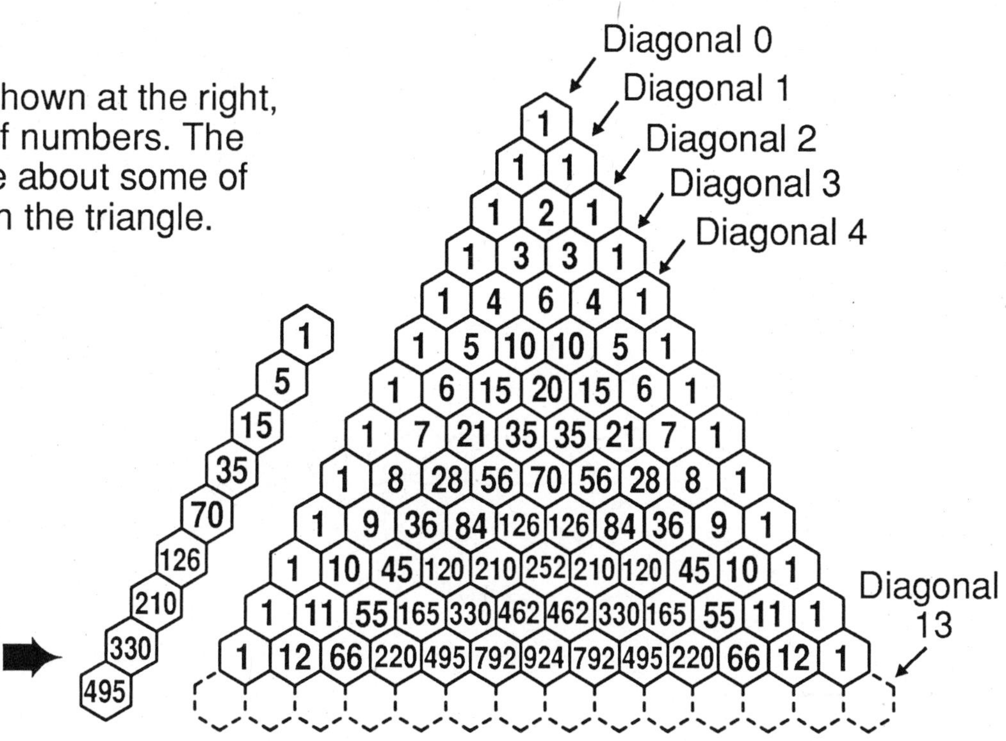

Diagonal 0
Diagonal 1
Diagonal 2
Diagonal 3
Diagonal 4

```
                    1
                  1   1
                1   2   1
              1   3   3   1
            1   4   6   4   1
          1   5  10  10   5   1
        1   6  15  20  15   6   1
      1   7  21  35  35  21   7   1
    1   8  28  56  70  56  28   8   1
  1   9  36  84 126 126  84  36   9   1
1  10  45 120 210 252 210 120  45  10   1
1  11  55 165 330 462 462 330 165  55  11   1
1  12  66 220 495 792 924 792 495 220  66  12   1
```

Fourth diagonal in Pascal's Triangle ➡

1
5
15
35
70
126
210
330
495

Diagonal 13

---

1. The outside diagonal of 1's is considered the 0th diagonal. Which diagonal shows the counting numbers?

2. Which diagonal displays the sum of consecutive counting numbers?

---

3. Where do you find powers of 11 in the triangle?

4. $11^5 = 161,051$. Which row in the triangle should this be?

---

5. Find and describe some patterns of your own:

SQUARE DOT PAPER AREAS ◆◆

1. Find the area of each set of figures on square dot paper.

Number of Dots Touched (D)	Number of Dots Within (W)	Area in Square Units (A)	
3	0	$\frac{1}{2}$	
4	0	1	
5	0	___	
___	___	___	

2. Use your results from above. Draw a ring around the correct formula below.

$A = D + W$ $A = \frac{D}{2} + W$ $A = \frac{D}{2} - 1 + W$ $A = \frac{D}{2} + 1 + W$

3. Find the area of each set of figures on square dot paper.

	(D)	(W)	(A)
	3	1	___
	4	1	___
	___	___	___
	___	___	___

4. Use your results from above. Draw a ring around the correct formula below.

$A = D + W$ $A = \frac{D}{2} + W$ $A = \frac{D}{2} - 1 + W$ $A = \frac{D}{2} + 1 + W$

5. Use square dot paper to draw polygons having two inside dots. What formula will relate A, D, and W?

6. Perform the same experiment with three inside dots. What formula will relate A, D, and W?

CRITICAL THINKING ACTIVITIES IN PATTERNS, IMAGERY, LOGIC (Secondary)
© Dale Seymour Publications

BINGO PATTERNS (I)

◆◆

Five in a row make a BINGO.
Mark a BINGO of multiples of 3 by drawing a ring around each.
Mark a BINGO of multiples of 8 by putting an X on each.
Mark a BINGO of multiples of both 2 and 7. Draw a line through them.

1.

B	I	N	G	O
8	21	33	60	75
9	16	32	48	64
7	18	free	54	69
14	28	42	56	70
6	24	48	50	72

2.

B	I	N	G	O
6	27	42	57	65
14	28	49	51	70
9	21	free	60	62
8	24	33	48	64
3	16	32	54	66

NUMBER PATTERNS (II)

◆◆

Look at the numbers in each shape. What do the numbers have in common?

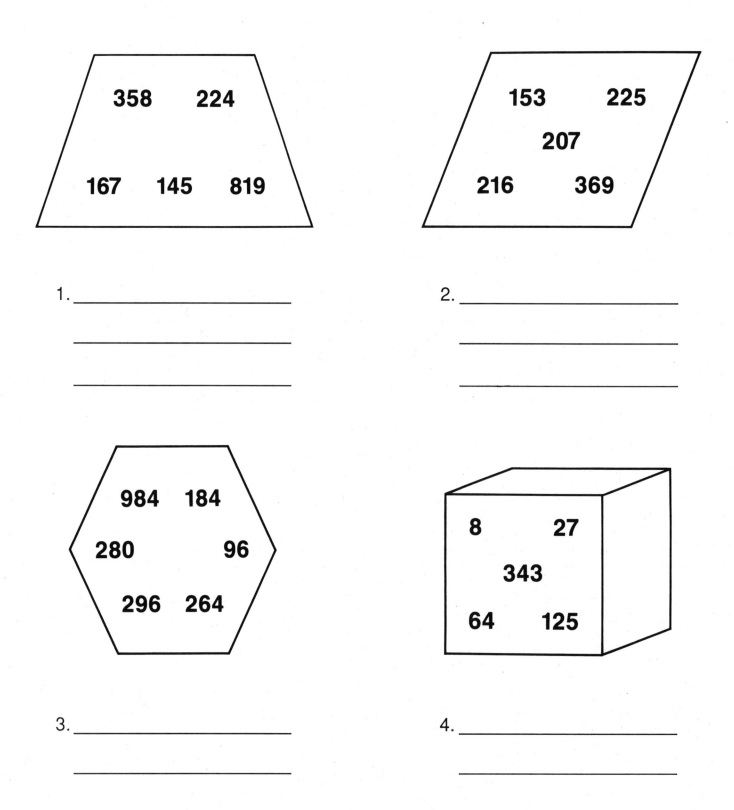

358   224

167   145   819

1. _____

_____

_____

153   225

207

216   369

2. _____

_____

_____

984   184

280   96

296   264

3. _____

_____

8   27

343

64   125

4. _____

_____

CRITICAL THINKING ACTIVITIES IN PATTERNS, IMAGERY, LOGIC (Secondary)
© Dale Seymour Publications

GEOMETRIC PATTERNS

◆◆

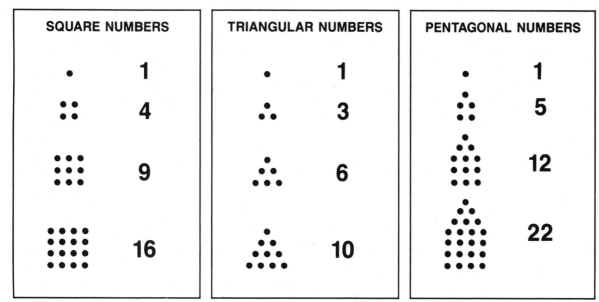

SQUARE NUMBERS	TRIANGULAR NUMBERS	PENTAGONAL NUMBERS
1	1	1
4	3	5
9	6	12
16	10	22

Study the charts above to answer these questions.

1. What is the third triangular number? _____

2. What is the fifth triangular number? _____

3. What is the fourth square number? _____

4. What is the fifth square number? _____

5. What is the tenth square number? _____

6. Draw a straight line that separates the sixteen dots in the square number example into two triangular numbers.

7. Divide the nine dots into two triangular numbers.

8. The third square number equals the sum of the _____ and _____ triangular numbers.

9. The fourth square number equals the sum of the _____ and _____ triangular numbers.

10. The third pentagonal number equals the sum of the second _____ number and the _____ square number.

11. The fourth pentagonal number equals the sum of the _____ number and the _____ number.

12. The tenth square number equals the sum of the _____ _____.

13. The 100th pentagonal number equals the sum of the _____ _____.

WINNER PATTERNS (I)

In Round 1, player 3 wins the match against player 4. Round 2 begins. Player 3 then goes on to play the winner of the match between players 15 and 12.

Study the numbers and find out who wins each match. Then look at the number pattern determined by the winners.

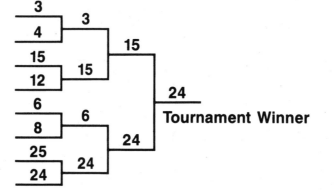

Who always wins? _____

Now do the same for Tournament 2.

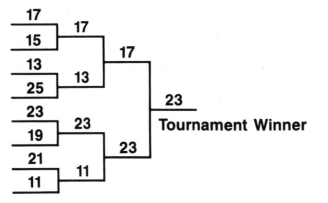

Who always wins? _____

CRITICAL THINKING ACTIVITIES IN PATTERNS, IMAGERY, LOGIC (Secondary)

NUMBER PATTERNS (III)

◆◆

1. Complete and extend each pattern:

Set 1	Set 2
9 + 9 = ___	9 x 9 = ___
24 + 3 = ___	24 x 3 = ___
47 + 2 = ___	47 x 2 = ___
497 + 2 = ___	497 x 2 = ___
4,997 + 2 = ___	4,997 x 2 = ___
49,997 + 2 = ___	49,997 x 2 = ___
___ + ___ = ___	___ x 2 = ___
___ + ___ = ___	___ x 2 = ___

Compare the two sets of patterns. Describe your results:

_____

_____

2. Extend this pattern:

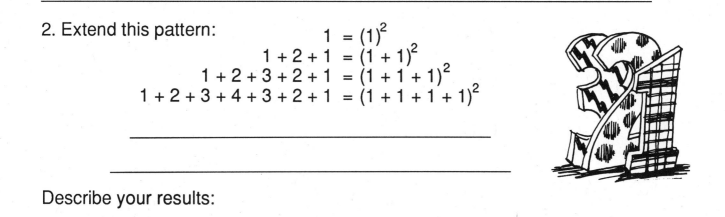

$$1 = (1)^2$$
$$1 + 2 + 1 = (1 + 1)^2$$
$$1 + 2 + 3 + 2 + 1 = (1 + 1 + 1)^2$$
$$1 + 2 + 3 + 4 + 3 + 2 + 1 = (1 + 1 + 1 + 1)^2$$

_____

_____

Describe your results:

_____

_____

3. Extend this pattern:

$$1 \times 2 \times 3 \times 4 + 1 = 25 = 5^2$$
$$2 \times 3 \times 4 \times 5 + 1 = 121 = 11^2$$
$$3 \times 4 \times 5 \times 6 + 1 = \underline{\quad} = \underline{\quad}$$
$$4 \times 5 \times 6 \times 7 + 1 = \underline{\quad} = \underline{\quad}$$

_____

_____

Describe your results:

_____

_____

4. Extend this pattern:

$$1^2 + 2^2 + 2^2 = 9 = 3^2$$
$$2^2 + 3^2 + 6^2 = 49 = 7^2$$
$$3^2 + 4^2 + 12^2 = \underline{\quad} = \underline{\quad}$$
$$4^2 + 5^2 + 20^2 = \underline{\quad} = \underline{\quad}$$

_____

_____

Describe your results:

_____

_____

HUNDREDS CHART PATTERNS (II) ◆◆

Mentally place each box-and-circle figure on the chart so that a number is in each box and circle. Add the numbers in the boxes and record the sum. Add the numbers in the circles and multiply that number by 3. Record the answer. What do you notice?

0	1	2	3	4	5	6	7	8	9
10	11	12	13	14	15	16	17	18	19
20	21	22	23	24	25	26	27	28	29
30	31	32	33	34	35	36	37	38	39
40	41	42	43	44	45	46	47	48	49
50	51	52	53	54	55	56	57	58	59
60	61	62	63	64	65	66	67	68	69
70	71	72	73	74	75	76	77	78	79
80	81	82	83	84	85	86	87	88	89
90	91	92	93	94	95	96	97	98	99

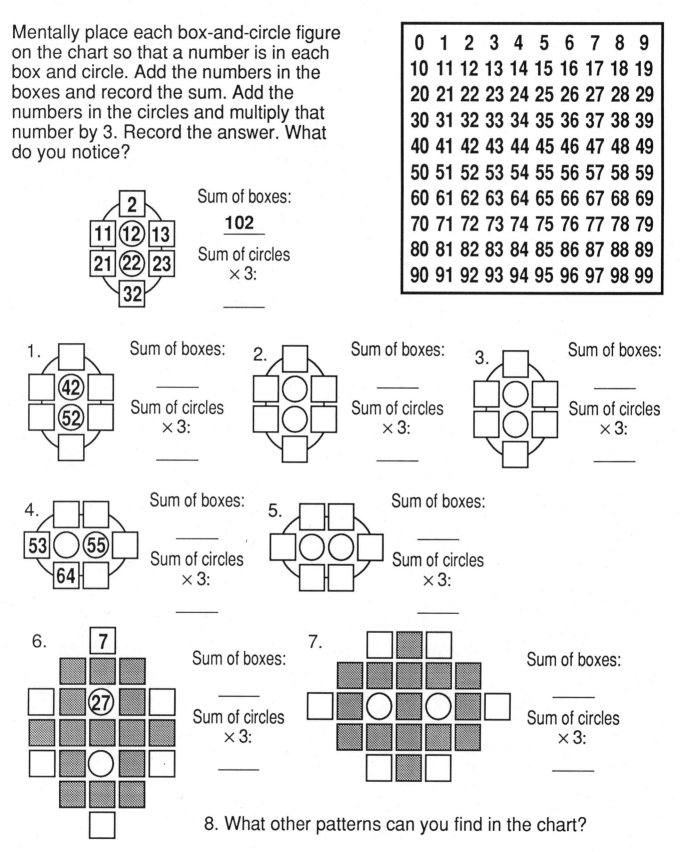

Sum of boxes:

102

Sum of circles × 3:
_____

1.

Sum of boxes:
_____

Sum of circles × 3:
_____

2.

Sum of boxes:
_____

Sum of circles × 3:
_____

3.

Sum of boxes:
_____

Sum of circles × 3:
_____

4.

Sum of boxes:
_____

Sum of circles × 3:
_____

5.

Sum of boxes:
_____

Sum of circles × 3:
_____

6.

Sum of boxes:
_____

Sum of circles × 3:
_____

7.

Sum of boxes:
_____

Sum of circles × 3:
_____

8. What other patterns can you find in the chart?

CRITICAL THINKING ACTIVITIES IN PATTERNS, IMAGERY, LOGIC (Secondary)

ADDITION TABLE PATTERNS (II)

◆◆

Mentally place the box-and-circle figure on the chart so that a number is in each box and circle. Add the numbers in the boxes and record the sum. Add the numbers in the circles and multiply that number by 3. Record the answer. What do you notice?

+	0	1	2	3	4	5	6	7	8	9
0	0	1	2	3	4	5	6	7	8	9
1	1	2	3	4	5	6	7	8	9	10
2	2	3	4	5	6	7	8	9	10	11
3	3	4	5	6	7	8	9	10	11	12
4	4	5	6	7	8	9	10	11	12	13
5	5	6	7	8	9	10	11	12	13	14
6	6	7	8	9	10	11	12	13	14	15
7	7	8	9	10	11	12	13	14	15	16
8	8	9	10	11	12	13	14	15	16	17
9	9	10	11	12	13	14	15	16	17	18

Sum of boxes:

33

Sum of circles × 3:

_____

1. Sum of boxes:

_____

Sum of circles × 3:

_____

2. Sum of boxes:

_____

Sum of circles × 3:

_____

3. Sum of boxes:

_____

Sum of circles × 3:

_____

4. Sum of boxes:

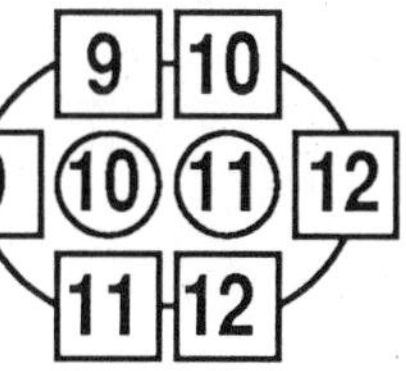

_____

Sum of circles × 3:

_____

5. Sum of boxes:

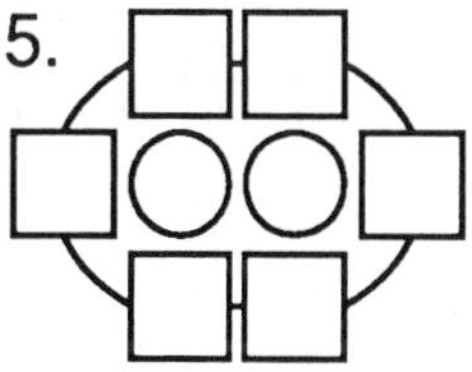

_____

Sum of circles × 3:

_____

6. Sum of boxes:

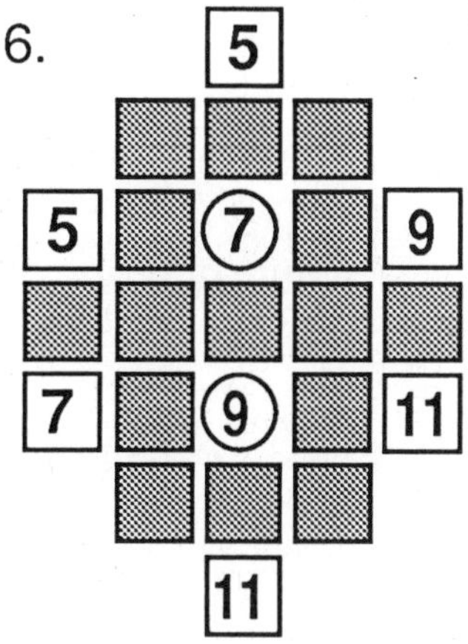

_____

Sum of circles × 3:

_____

7. Sum of boxes:

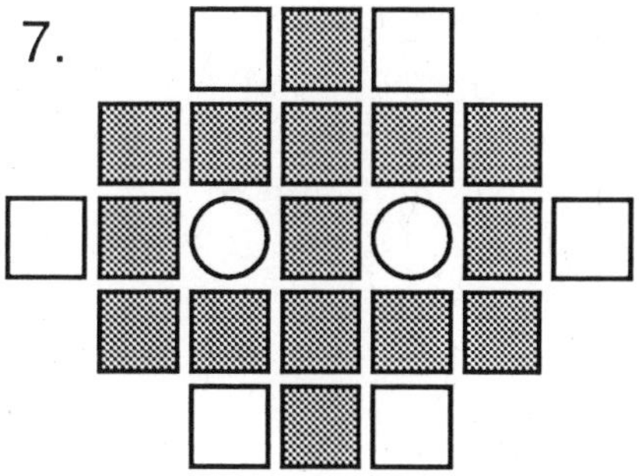

_____

Sum of circles × 3:

_____

8. What other patterns can you find in the chart?

MULTIPLICATION TABLE PATTERNS (II) ◆◆

Mentally place the box-and-circle figure on the chart so that a number is in each box and circle. Add the numbers in the boxes and record the sum. Add the numbers in the circles and multiply that number by 3. Record the answer. What do you notice?

×	0	1	2	3	4	5	6	7	8	9
0	0	0	0	0	0	0	0	0	0	0
1	0	1	2	3	4	5	6	7	8	9
2	0	2	4	6	8	10	12	14	16	18
3	0	3	6	9	12	15	18	21	24	27
4	0	4	8	12	16	20	24	28	32	36
5	0	5	10	15	20	25	30	35	40	45
6	0	6	12	18	24	30	36	42	48	54
7	0	7	14	21	28	35	42	49	56	63
8	0	8	16	24	32	40	48	56	64	72
9	0	9	18	27	36	45	54	63	72	81

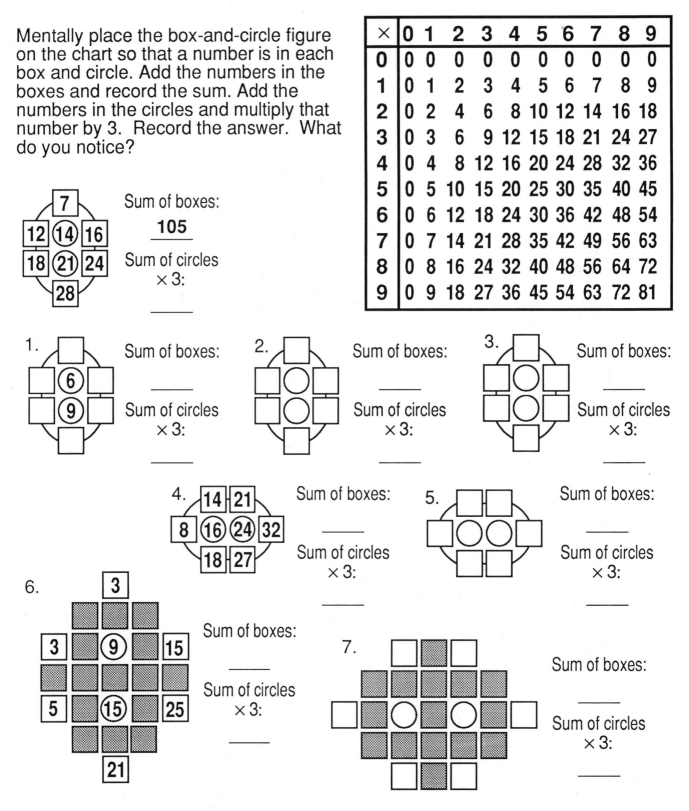

Sum of boxes:

105

Sum of circles × 3:
_____

1. Sum of boxes: _____ Sum of circles × 3: _____

2. Sum of boxes: _____ Sum of circles × 3: _____

3. Sum of boxes: _____ Sum of circles × 3: _____

4. Sum of boxes: _____ Sum of circles × 3: _____

5. Sum of boxes: _____ Sum of circles × 3: _____

6. Sum of boxes: _____ Sum of circles × 3: _____

7. Sum of boxes: _____ Sum of circles × 3: _____

8. What other patterns can you find in the chart?

CRITICAL THINKING ACTIVITIES IN PATTERNS, IMAGERY, LOGIC (Secondary)
© Dale Seymour Publications

POLYHEDRON PATTERNS

◆◆◆

Count and record the number of faces (F), vertices (V), and edges (E) for each polyhedron. Then calculate the values for F + V – E.

NAME	FIGURE	FACES (F)	VERTICES (V)	EDGES (E)	F + V – E
Tetrahedron		_4_	_4_	_6_	_4 + 4 – 6 = 2_
Hexahedron (cube)		___	___	___	___
Octahedron		___	___	___	___
Dodecahedron		___	___	___	___
Icosahedron		___	___	___	___

1. What pattern did you observe in the last column?

2. Determine whether or not this relationship holds with an ordinary box (rectangular prism).

3. Explore this relationship with another polyhedron that has faces, vertices, and edges but is not a rectangular prism.

ODD INTEGER PATTERNS

◆◆◆

It is often helpful in mathematics to look for patterns that will lead to time-saving shortcuts. Some patterns are shown below.

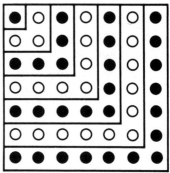

Write each sum.

1. 1 = _____
2. 1 + 3 = _____
3. 1 + 3 + 5 = _____
4. 1 + 3 + 5 + 7 = _____
5. 1 + 3 + 5 + 7+ 9 = _____
6. 1 + 3 + 5 + 7 + 9 + 11 = _____
7. 1 + 3 + 5 + 7+ 9 + 11 + 13 = _____
8. What do the sums have in common?_____
9. Describe a general rule that may be true and that is
   illustrated by the examples above._____

_____

Write the number of terms in each series: (The symbol; "..." means that the pattern continues.)

10. 1 + 3 + 5: _____ terms

11. 1 + 3 + 5 + 7: _____ terms

12. 1 + 3 + 5 + 7+ 9: _____ terms

13. 1 + 3 + 5 + 7 + 9 + 11: _____ terms

14. 1 + 3 + 5 + 7+ 9 + 11 + 13: _____ terms

15. 1 + 3 + 5 + ... + 19 + 21: _____ terms

16. 1 + 3 + 5 + ... + 29 + 31: _____ terms

17. 1 + 3 + 5 + ... + 57 + 59: _____ terms

18. 1 + 3 + 5 + ... + 97 + 99: _____ terms

19. What pattern or rule can you find that will help find the number of
    terms in the series?_____

_____

Use the two rules to find the following sums:

20. 1 + 3 + ... + 47 + 49 = _____

21. 1 + 3 + ... + 57 + 59 = _____

22. 1 + 3 + ... + 97 + 99 = _____

23. 1 + 3 + ... + 121 + 123 = _____

24. 1 + 3 + ... + 185 + 187 = _____

25. 1 + 3 + ... + 397 + 399 = _____

CRITICAL THINKING ACTIVITIES IN PATTERNS, IMAGERY, LOGIC (Secondary)
© Dale Seymour Publications

FAREY SEQUENCES

◆◆◆

A Farey sequence is one in which F_n is defined as the ordered set of all proper fractions with denominators of 2 to n.

A Farey sequence can be written in two steps:
Step 1: Write all proper fractions with denominators of 2 to n.
Step 2: Order the fractions from smallest to largest. (Write equivalent fractions one time only.)

Examples:

F_1: no sequence

F_2: *Step 1:* $\frac{1}{2}$ *Step 2:* $\frac{1}{2}$

F_3: *Step 1:* $\frac{1}{2}, \frac{1}{3}, \frac{2}{3}$ *Step 2:* $\frac{1}{3}, \frac{1}{2}, \frac{2}{3}$

F_4: *Step 1:* $\frac{1}{2}, \frac{1}{3}, \frac{2}{3}, \frac{1}{4}, \frac{2}{4}, \frac{3}{4}$ *Step 2:* $\frac{1}{4}, \frac{1}{3}, \frac{1}{2}, \frac{2}{3}, \frac{3}{4}$

Write the following Farey sequences:

Step 1	*Step 2*
F_5: _____	_____
_____	_____
F_6: _____	_____
_____	_____
_____	_____
F_7: _____	_____
_____	_____
_____	_____
_____	_____

PATTERNS IN FAREY SEQUENCES

Study the pattern for sequence F_4 below. Then complete the chart.

Sequence	Fraction	Two Neighbors of the Fraction	Sum of Numerators and Denominators
F_4	$\dfrac{2}{3}$	$\dfrac{1}{2}, \dfrac{3}{4}$	$\dfrac{1+3}{2+4} = \dfrac{4}{6} = \dfrac{2}{3}$
F_5	$\dfrac{2}{5}$	$\dfrac{1}{3}, \dfrac{1}{2}$	_____
F_5	$\dfrac{2}{3}$	_____	_____
F_6	$\dfrac{4}{5}$	_____	_____
F_7	$\dfrac{2}{3}$	_____	_____

Describe the general pattern for "neighbors" in a Farey sequence:

Study the pattern for sequence F_4 below. Then complete the chart.

Sequence	Sum of Pairs of Fractions Equidistant from $\frac{1}{2}$	
F_4	$\dfrac{1}{3} + \dfrac{2}{3} = 1$	$\dfrac{1}{4} + \dfrac{3}{4} = 1$
F_5	_____	_____
F_6	_____	_____
F_7	_____	_____

Describe the general pattern for the sum of fraction pairs equidistant from $\dfrac{1}{2}$:

CRITICAL THINKING ACTIVITIES IN PATTERNS, IMAGERY, LOGIC (Secondary)
© Dale Seymour Publications

DIVISION PATTERNS

Work through the steps in the division problems below. Look for patterns.

1.
Start with two numbers:	0.125 and 0.2				
Divide the second by the first:	0.2	÷	0.125	=	1.6
Divide the answer by the number above it:	1.6	÷	0.2	=	8
Divide the answer by the number above it:	8	÷	1.6	=	5
Divide the answer by the number above it:	5	÷	8	=	0.625
Continue the process:	_____	÷	_____	=	_____
	_____	÷	_____	=	_____

What do you observe?

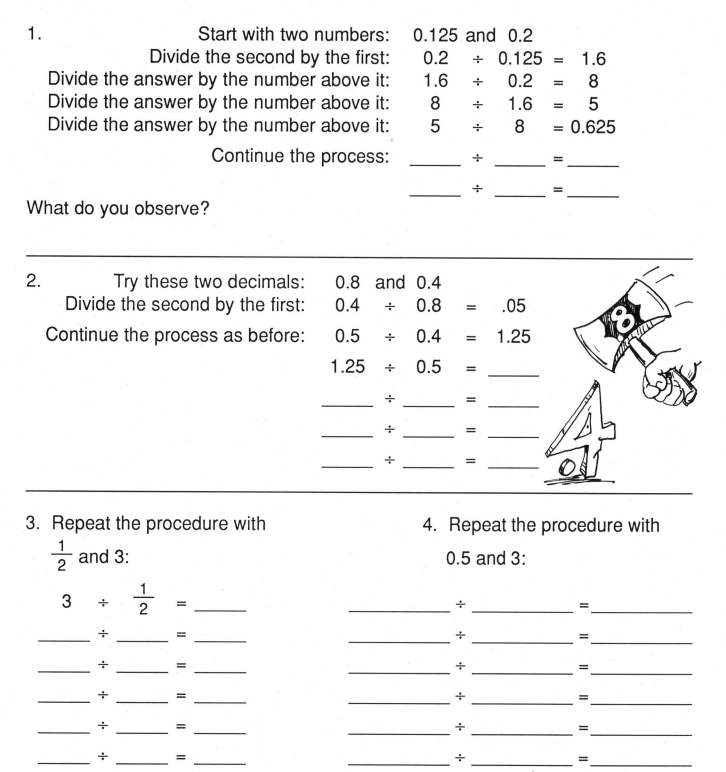

2.
Try these two decimals:	0.8 and 0.4				
Divide the second by the first:	0.4	÷	0.8	=	.05
Continue the process as before:	0.5	÷	0.4	=	1.25
	1.25	÷	0.5	=	_____
	_____	÷	_____	=	_____
	_____	÷	_____	=	_____
	_____	÷	_____	=	_____

3. Repeat the procedure with $\frac{1}{2}$ and 3:

$$3 \div \frac{1}{2} = \underline{\hspace{1cm}}$$

_____ ÷ _____ = _____

_____ ÷ _____ = _____

_____ ÷ _____ = _____

_____ ÷ _____ = _____

_____ ÷ _____ = _____

4. Repeat the procedure with 0.5 and 3:

_____ ÷ _____ = _____

_____ ÷ _____ = _____

_____ ÷ _____ = _____

_____ ÷ _____ = _____

_____ ÷ _____ = _____

_____ ÷ _____ = _____

5. On the back of this page, compare the results of problems 3 and 4.

DOODLING

Doodle 1

Doodle 2

Shade in Doodle 3

Join the dots to draw Doodle 4. Then shade it.

Draw doodle 5 here.

1. How many squares are there in:

Doodle 1? ___ Doodle 2? ___ Doodle 3? ___

Doodle 4? ___ Doodle 5? ___ Doodle 6? ___

Doodle 10? ___

2. How many triangles are there in:

Doodle 1? ___ Doodle 2? ___ Doodle 3? ___

Doodle 4? ___ Doodle 5? ___ Doodle 6? ___

Doodle 10? ___

3. Predict how many squares would be in Doodle 100:

4. Write the general rule for how many squares are in the
   n th doodle:

SUCCESSIVE DECREASES AND INCREASES   ◆◆◆

Study the example below. Then complete the following columns. *Example:*

Start with: **100.**
After a 10% decrease, you get: 100 − (10% x 100) = **90.**
After a 10% increase, you get: 90 + (10% x 90) = **99.**
The net increase/decrease is : 100 − 99 = **1.**
The net change (%) is: 1/100 = **1% decrease**.

	% Decrease	% Increase	Net Change
1.	10	10	1% decrease
2.	20	20	_____
3.	30	30	_____
4.	20	40	_____
5.	50	80	_____

	% Increase	% Decrease	Net Change
6.	10	10	1% decrease
7.	10	20	_____
8.	20	20	_____
9.	20	10	_____
10.	20	40	_____

Complete these statements:

11. A decrease followed by an equivalent increase results in_____.
    (a decrease or an increase?)

12. An increase followed by an equivalent decrease results in_____.
    (a decrease or an increase?)

CHART AND TABLE PATTERNS

◆◆◆

Mentally place the box-and-circle figures shown below on the charts so that a number is in each box and circle.

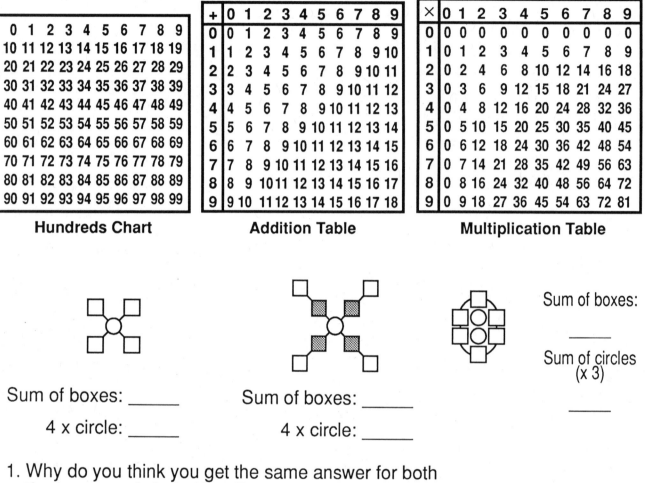

	0	1	2	3	4	5	6	7	8	9
0	1	2	3	4	5	6	7	8	9
10	11	12	13	14	15	16	17	18	19
20	21	22	23	24	25	26	27	28	29
30	31	32	33	34	35	36	37	38	39
40	41	42	43	44	45	46	47	48	49
50	51	52	53	54	55	56	57	58	59
60	61	62	63	64	65	66	67	68	69
70	71	72	73	74	75	76	77	78	79
80	81	82	83	84	85	86	87	88	89
90	91	92	93	94	95	96	97	98	99

Hundreds Chart

+	0	1	2	3	4	5	6	7	8	9
0	0	1	2	3	4	5	6	7	8	9
1	1	2	3	4	5	6	7	8	9	10
2	2	3	4	5	6	7	8	9	10	11
3	3	4	5	6	7	8	9	10	11	12
4	4	5	6	7	8	9	10	11	12	13
5	5	6	7	8	9	10	11	12	13	14
6	6	7	8	9	10	11	12	13	14	15
7	7	8	9	10	11	12	13	14	15	16
8	8	9	10	11	12	13	14	15	16	17
9	9	10	11	12	13	14	15	16	17	18

Addition Table

×	0	1	2	3	4	5	6	7	8	9
0	0	0	0	0	0	0	0	0	0	0
1	0	1	2	3	4	5	6	7	8	9
2	0	2	4	6	8	10	12	14	16	18
3	0	3	6	9	12	15	18	21	24	27
4	0	4	8	12	16	20	24	28	32	36
5	0	5	10	15	20	25	30	35	40	45
6	0	6	12	18	24	30	36	42	48	54
7	0	7	14	21	28	35	42	49	56	63
8	0	8	16	24	32	40	48	56	64	72
9	0	9	18	27	36	45	54	63	72	81

Multiplication Table

Sum of boxes: _____

4 x circle: _____

Sum of boxes: _____

4 x circle: _____

Sum of boxes:

_____

Sum of circles
(x 3)

_____

1. Why do you think you get the same answer for both the boxes and circles in a figure no matter what chart you select?

2. Create your own rectangular pattern that has a center number. Test your pattern on any of the three charts to see how that center number relates to the sum of the four corner numbers. What is the pattern?

3. Can you create a triangular pattern of numbers in which the center number always has the same relationship to the sum of the three corner numbers? Test it on all three charts.

4. What other patterns can you find?

CRITICAL THINKING ACTIVITIES IN PATTERNS, IMAGERY, LOGIC (Secondary)
© Dale Seymour Publications

DIFFERENCE PATTERNS

Complete each table. Write the rule and find the difference of successive *y* values.

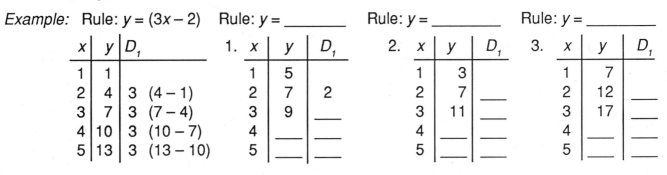

Example: Rule: $y = (3x - 2)$

x	y	D₁
1	1	
2	4	3 (4 − 1)
3	7	3 (7 − 4)
4	10	3 (10 − 7)
5	13	3 (13 − 10)

Rule: $y =$ _____

1.
x	y	D₁
1	5	
2	7	2
3	9	_
4	_	_
5	_	_

Rule: $y =$ _____

2.
x	y	D₁
1	3	
2	7	_
3	11	_
4	_	_
5	_	_

Rule: $y =$ _____

3.
x	y	D₁
1	7	
2	12	_
3	17	_
4	_	_
5	_	_

Now find D_1 (difference of y's) and D_2 (difference of D_1) for these quadratic relations.

Example: Rule: $y = x^2 + 1$

x	y	D₁	D₂
1	2		
2	5	3	
3	10	5	2
4	17	7	2
5	26	9	2

Rule: $y =$ _____

4.
x	y	D₁	D₂
1	4		
2	10	_	
3	20	_	_
4	34	_	_
5	_	_	_

Rule: $y =$ _____

5.
x	y	D₁	D₂
1	2		
2	11	_	
3	26	_	_
4	47	_	_
5	_	_	_

Rule: $y =$ _____

6.
x	y	D₁	D₂
1	1		
2	13	_	
3	33	_	_
4	61	_	_
5	_	_	_

Now find D_1, D_2, and D_3.

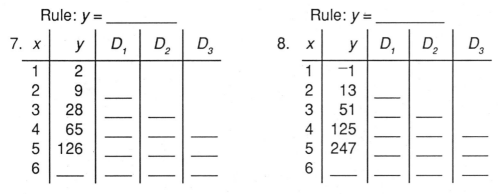

Rule: $y =$ _____

7.
x	y	D₁	D₂	D₃
1	2			
2	9	_		
3	28	_	_	
4	65	_	_	_
5	126	_	_	_
6	_	_	_	_

Rule: $y =$ _____

8.
x	y	D₁	D₂	D₃
1	−1			
2	13	_		
3	51	_	_	
4	125	_	_	_
5	247	_	_	_
6	_	_	_	_

Use your results to complete the following statements:

9. In a rule where the highest power of *x* is 1 then the first differences are

   _____.

10. In a rule where the highest power of *x* is 2 then the second differences

    are _____.

11. In a rule where the highest power of *x* is 3 then the _____

    differences are _____.

DIAGONAL PATTERNS

◆◆◆

A diagonal of a polygon joins two non-adjacent vertices. Find the total number of diagonals in the following polygons using the diagrams below and your problem-solving skills.

1. seven sides _____   2. eight sides _____   3. nine sides _____

4. ten sides _____   5. twelve sides _____   6. eighteen sides _____

7. one hundred sides _____   8. *n* sides _____

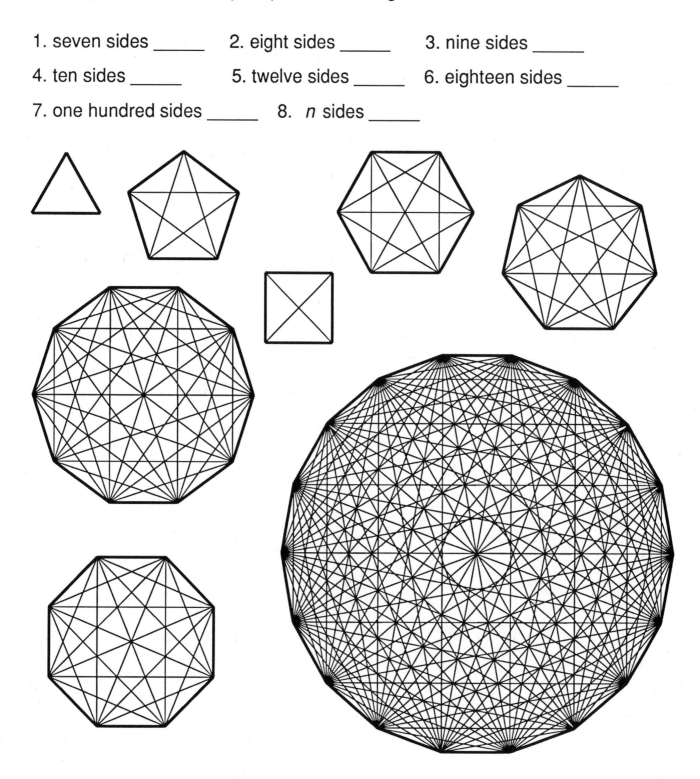

CRITICAL THINKING ACTIVITIES IN PATTERNS, IMAGERY, LOGIC (Secondary)
© Dale Seymour Publications

SEQUENCE PATTERNS

Fill in the blanks in each of the problems below. Use your
answers to find number patterns. Describe the patterns
you discover in words and/or in equations. Compare your
descriptions with classmates'.

1

1   2   3   4   5   6   7   8   9   . . .

1   3   6   10   15   ___   ___   ___   ___

Describe a pattern:

2

1   3   5   7   9   11   13   15   17   . . .

1   4   9   ___   ___   ___   ___   ___   ___

Describe a pattern:

3

2   4   6   8   10   12   14   16   18   . . .

___   ___   ___   ___   ___   ___   ___

Describe a pattern:

4

1   3   5   7   9   11   13   15   17   19

___   ___   ___   ___

Describe a pattern:

5

1   2   3   4   5   6   7   8   9   10   11   12   13   14   15   . . .

___   ___   ___   ___   ___

Describe a pattern:

COUNTING DOT PATTERNS

The first four terms of some patterns of dots are shown below.
Look for number patterns that would give a rule to help find
the fifth, tenth, and *n*th terms in the sequence.

1.
  a. How many dots in the fifth term? _____

b. How many dots in
    the tenth term? _____

c. How many dots in
    the *n*th term? _____

2.
  a. How many dots in the fifth term? _____

b. How many dots in
    the tenth term? _____

c. How many dots in
    the *n*th term? _____

3.
  a. How many dots in the
    fifth term? _____

b. How many dots in
    the tenth term? _____

c. How many dots in
    the *n*th term? _____

4.
  a. How many dots in the fifth term? _____

b. How many dots in
    the tenth term? _____

c. How many dots in
    the *n*th term? _____

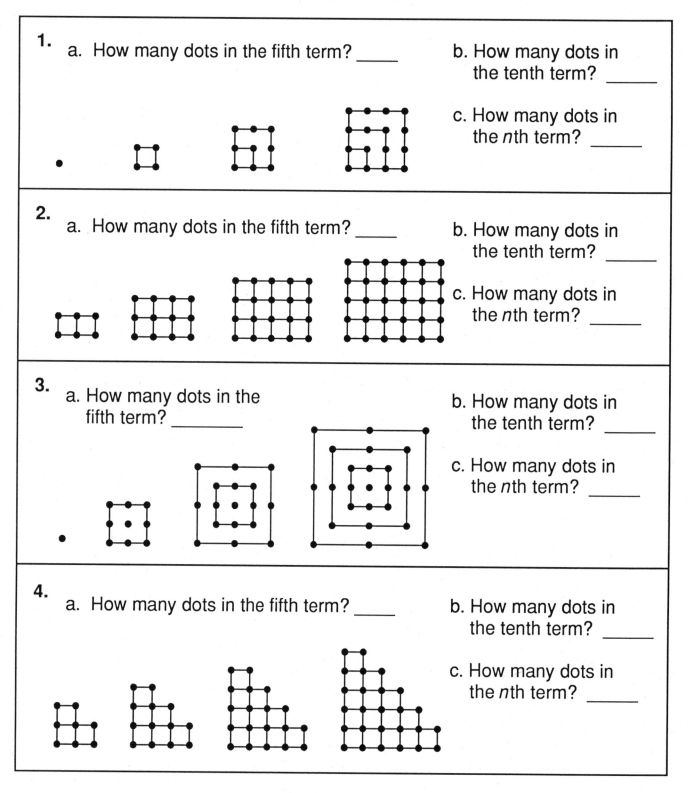

CRITICAL THINKING ACTIVITIES IN PATTERNS, IMAGERY, LOGIC (Secondary)
© Dale Seymour Publications

BINGO PATTERNS (II)

Five in a row make a BINGO.
Mark a BINGO of even multiples of 3 by drawing a ring around each.
Mark a BINGO of multiples of 5 by drawing a line through them.
Mark a BINGO of prime numbers by putting an X on each.
Mark a BINGO of odd composite numbers by drawing a star on each.

1.

B	I	N	G	O
10	29	41	53	71
12	20	37	47	63
5	15	free	54	66
1	23	43	55	75
11	30	39	59	72

2.

B	I	N	G	O
5	29	41	56	70
9	25	45	57	69
7	17	free	51	71
12	30	42	60	72
6	24	36	48	75

CUTTING A CAKE ◆◆◆

Cut a cake with straight cuts to get the greatest number of pieces. Draw the pattern for three and four cuts—and fill in the chart. Cuts do not necessarily have to slice the top and bottom of the cake.

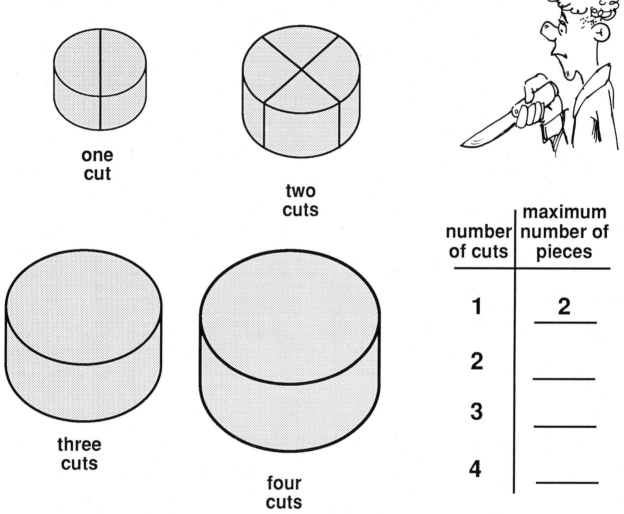

number of cuts	maximum number of pieces
1	2
2	
3	
4	

Additional Activities:

Visualizing the cuts for four or more slices is difficult! A formula for finding the maximum number of pieces from n cuts is

$$\frac{n^3 + bn + c}{6}$$

where b and c are positive values. Use your chart to find b and c. Then use the formula to find the number of pieces from five cuts.

Class Challenge:

Construct a three-dimensional model showing the four-cut case.

CRITICAL THINKING ACTIVITIES IN PATTERNS, IMAGERY, LOGIC (Secondary)

WINNER PATTERNS (II)

In Round 1, player 40 wins the match against player 44. Round 2 begins. Player 40 then plays the winner of the match between players 46 and 48.

Study the numbers and find out who wins each match. Then look at the number pattern determined by the winners.

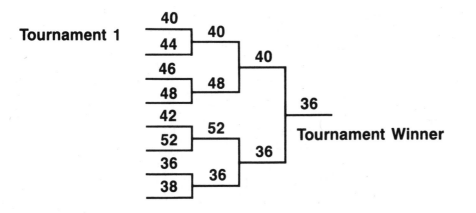

Tournament 1

```
40
44    40
          40
46
48    48
              40
42
52    52
          36
36
38    36
                  36
              Tournament Winner
```

Who always wins? _____

Challenge: Now do the same for Tournament 2.

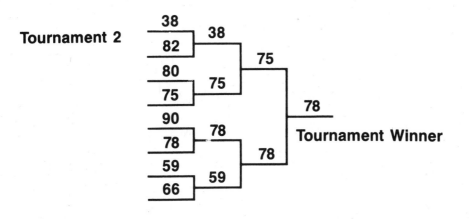

Tournament 2

```
38
82    38
          75
80
75    75
              78
90
78    78
          78
59
66    59
                  78
              Tournament Winner
```

Who always wins? _____

_____

CRITICAL THINKING ACTIVITIES IN PATTERNS, IMAGERY, AND LOGIC (Secondary)
© Dale Seymour Publications

NUMBER PATTERNS (IV)

1. Extend the pattern:

$$1^2 = 1$$
$$11^2 = 121$$
$$111^2 = 12,321$$
$$1,111^2 = 1,234,321$$

_____

_____

_____

When do you think this pattern might not continue?

_____

_____

2. Complete the pattern:

$$3^2 + 4^2 = 5^2$$
$$10^2 + 11^2 + 12^2 = 13^2 + \underline{}$$
$$21^2 + 22^2 + 23^2 + \underline{} = \underline{}$$

3. Complete the pattern:

$$1^2 - 0^2 = \underline{}$$
$$2^2 - 1^2 = \underline{}$$
$$3^2 - \underline{} = \underline{}$$
$$\underline{} = \underline{}$$

4. Compute each sum:

Pair One: $32^2 + 63^2 + 79^2 = \underline{}$ $23^2 + 36^2 + 97^2 = \underline{}$

Pair Two: $33^2 + 69^2 + 72^2 = \underline{}$ $33^2 + 96^2 + 27^2 = \underline{}$

Pair Three: $39^2 + 62^2 + 73^2 = \underline{}$ $93^2 + 26^2 + 37^2 = \underline{}$

Pair Four: $32^2 + 69^2 + 73^2 = \underline{}$ $23^2 + 96^2 + 37^2 = \underline{}$

Pair Five: $33^2 + 62^2 + 79^2 = \underline{}$ $33^2 + 26^2 + 97^2 = \underline{}$

Compare the sums in each pair. Describe your results.

5. Here is another unusual pattern:

$$(88 + 209) \times (88 + 209) = (297)^2 = \underline{}$$
$$(494 + 209) \times (494 + 209) = (\underline{})^2 = \underline{}$$
$$(998 + 001) \times (998 + 001) = (\underline{})^2 = \underline{}$$
$$(744 + 1,984) \times (744 + 1,984) = (\underline{})^2 = \underline{}$$
$$(494 + 1,729) \times (494 + 1,729) = (\underline{})^2 = \underline{}$$

Describe your results.

CRITICAL THINKING ACTIVITIES IN PATTERNS, IMAGERY, LOGIC (Secondary)
© Dale Seymour Publications

PATTERNS WITHIN PATTERNS

Mathematics is sometimes defined as the study of patterns. Most patterns contain patterns in themselves. The patterns of rhombi and trapezoids below contain patterns of points, lines, and shapes.

Study the patterns and fill in the missing information.

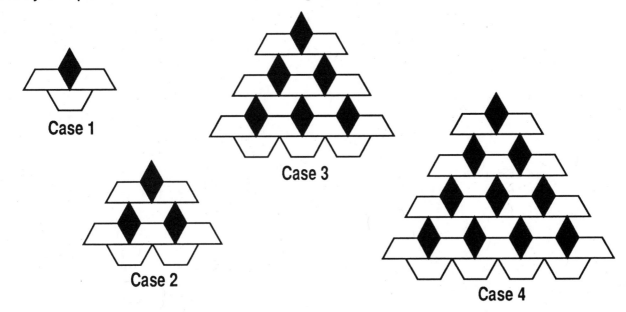

Case 1

Case 2

Case 3

Case 4

HOW MANY?	Case 1	Case 2	Case 3	Case 4	Case *n* or rule
Diamonds	1 or $\dfrac{1 \times 2}{2}$	3 or $\dfrac{2 \times 3}{2}$	6 or $\dfrac{3 \times 4}{2}$	___ or ___	$\dfrac{n(n+1)}{2}$
Trapezoids	3 or $2^2 - 1$	8 or $3^2 - 1$	___ or ___	___ or ___	
Non-overlapping polygons	4 or $\dfrac{1(3+5)}{2}$	11 or $\dfrac{2(6+5)}{2}$	___ or ___	___ or ___	
Vertices	12 or $1(2+9)+1$	___ or $2(4+9)+1$	___ or ___	___ or ___	
Quadrilateral edges *	16 or $\dfrac{4(3+5)}{2}$	___ or $\dfrac{8(6+5)}{2}$	___ or ___	___ or ___	

* Count shared edges twice.

CRITICAL THINKING ACTIVITIES IN PATTERNS, IMAGERY, LOGIC (Secondary)
© Dale Seymour Publications

HUNDREDS CHART (I)

0	1	2	3	4	5	6	7	8	9
10	11	12	13	14	15	16	17	18	19
20	21	22	23	24	25	26	27	28	29
30	31	32	33	34	35	36	37	38	39
40	41	42	43	44	45	46	47	48	49
50	51	52	53	54	55	56	57	58	59
60	61	62	63	64	65	66	67	68	69
70	71	72	73	74	75	76	77	78	79
80	81	82	83	84	85	86	87	88	89
90	91	92	93	94	95	96	97	98	99

1	2	3	4	5	6	7	8	9	10
11	12	13	14	15	16	17	18	19	20
21	22	23	24	25	26	27	28	29	30
31	32	33	34	35	36	37	38	39	40
41	42	43	44	45	46	47	48	49	50
51	52	53	54	55	56	57	58	59	60
61	62	63	64	65	66	67	68	69	70
71	72	73	74	75	76	77	78	79	80
81	82	83	84	85	86	87	88	89	90
91	92	93	94	95	96	97	98	99	100

ADDITION TABLE

+	1	2	3	4	5	6	7	8	9
1	2	3	4	5	6	7	8	9	10
2	3	4	5	6	7	8	9	10	11
3	4	5	6	7	8	9	10	11	12
4	5	6	7	8	9	10	11	12	13
5	6	7	8	9	10	11	12	13	14
6	7	8	9	10	11	12	13	14	15
7	8	9	10	11	12	13	14	15	16
8	9	10	11	12	13	14	15	16	17
9	10	11	12	13	14	15	16	17	18

MULTIPLICATION TABLE

×	1	2	3	4	5	6	7	8	9
1	1	2	3	4	5	6	7	8	9
2	2	4	6	8	10	12	14	16	18
3	3	6	9	12	15	18	21	24	27
4	4	8	12	16	20	24	28	32	36
5	5	10	15	20	25	30	35	40	45
6	6	12	18	24	30	36	42	48	54
7	7	14	21	28	35	42	49	56	63
8	8	16	24	32	40	48	56	64	72
9	9	18	27	36	45	54	63	72	81

CRITICAL THINKING ACTIVITIES IN PATTERNS, IMAGERY, AND LOGIC (Secondary)

PASCAL'S TRIANGLE

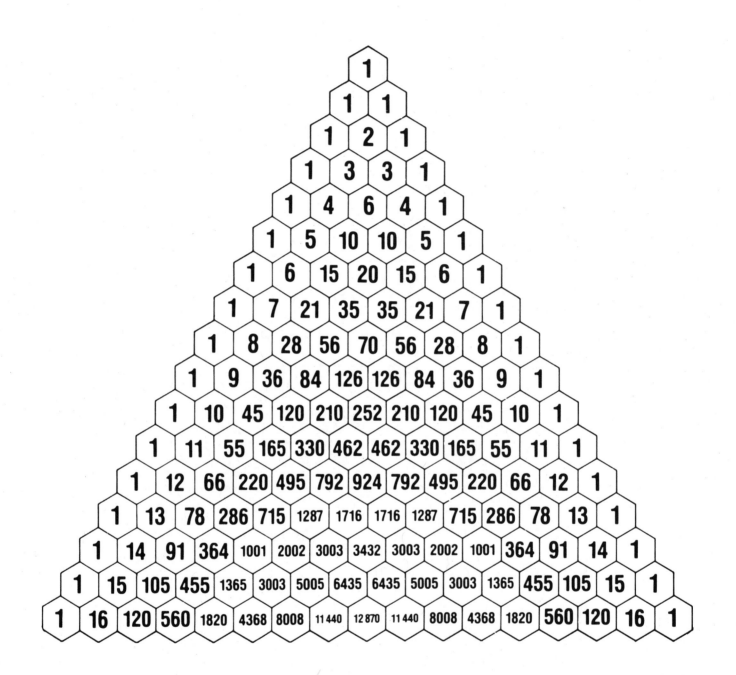

CRITICAL THINKING ACTIVITIES IN PATTERNS, IMAGERY, LOGIC (Secondary)
© Dale Seymour Publications

PART 2: IMAGERY

LETTER PUZZLE (I)

Compare the puzzle pieces with the lettered ones in the puzzle.
Write the correct letter on each piece.

CRITICAL THINKING ACTIVITIES IN PATTERNS, IMAGERY, LOGIC (Secondary)
© Dale Seymour Publications

OVERLAPPING FIGURES (I)

Three figures are overlapping in A, B, and C below. Only their outlines show. For each outline, draw in the lines showing the three figures.

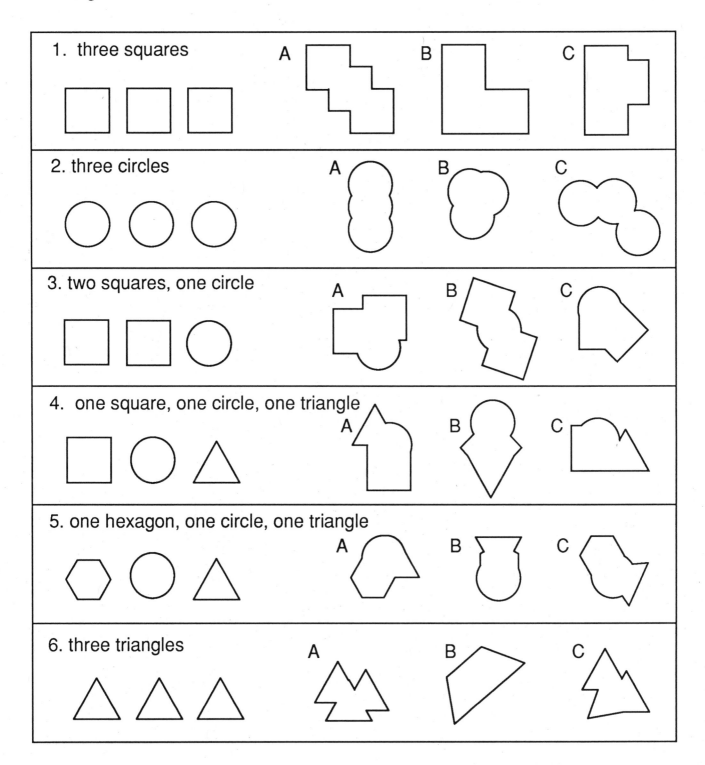

1. three squares   A   B   C

2. three circles   A   B   C

3. two squares, one circle   A   B   C

4. one square, one circle, one triangle   A   B   C

5. one hexagon, one circle, one triangle   A   B   C

6. three triangles   A   B   C

OVERLAPPING FIGURES (II)

The outlines below were produced by overlapping figures. Draw the figures and name them.

Choose from: square, equilateral triangle, circle, rhombus, regular pentagon, and regular hexagon.

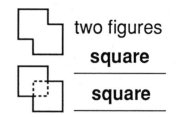

two figures

square

_____

square

_____

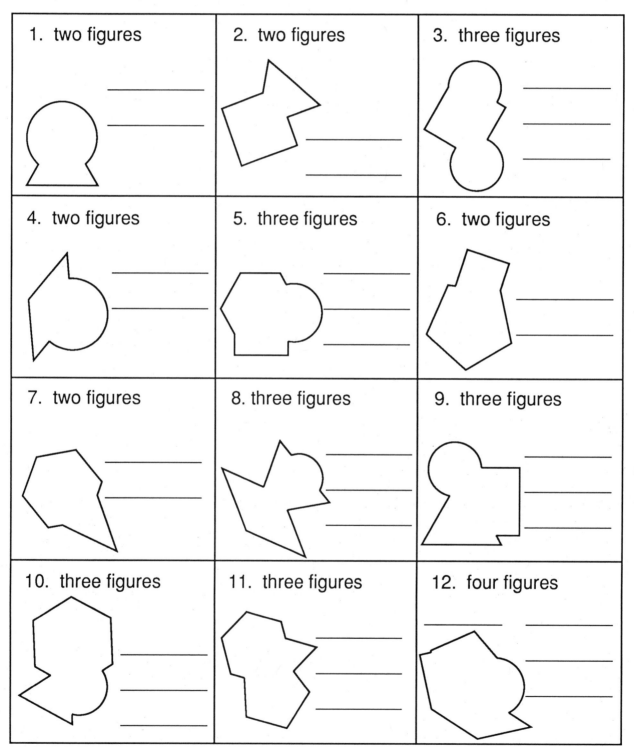

1. two figures _____

2. two figures _____ _____

3. three figures _____ _____ _____

4. two figures _____ _____

5. three figures _____ _____ _____

6. two figures _____ _____

7. two figures _____ _____

8. three figures _____ _____ _____

9. three figures _____ _____ _____

10. three figures _____ _____ _____

11. three figures _____ _____ _____

12. four figures _____ _____ _____ _____

CRITICAL THINKING ACTIVITIES IN PATTERNS, IMAGERY, LOGIC (Secondary)
© Dale Seymour Publications

DIRECTION CODES (I)

Write the direction code for each diagram below.

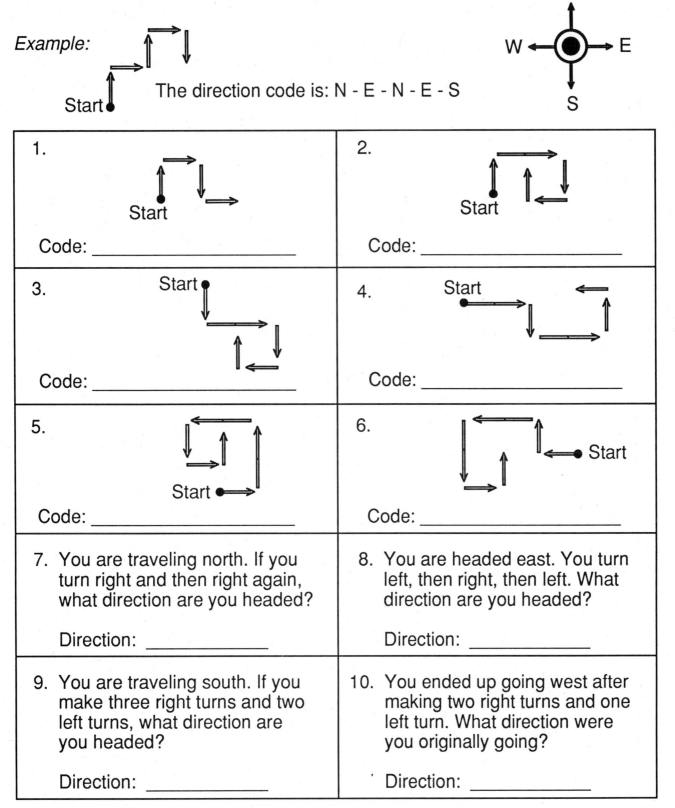

Example:

Start

The direction code is: N - E - N - E - S

1.

Start

Code: _____

2.

Start

Code: _____

3.

Start

Code: _____

4.

Start

Code: _____

5.

Start

Code: _____

6.

Start

Code: _____

7. You are traveling north. If you turn right and then right again, what direction are you headed?

Direction: _____

8. You are headed east. You turn left, then right, then left. What direction are you headed?

Direction: _____

9. You are traveling south. If you make three right turns and two left turns, what direction are you headed?

Direction: _____

10. You ended up going west after making two right turns and one left turn. What direction were you originally going?

Direction: _____

DIRECTION CODES (II)

Write the direction code for each diagram below.

Example:

The direction code is: N - NE - SE - S - SW - E

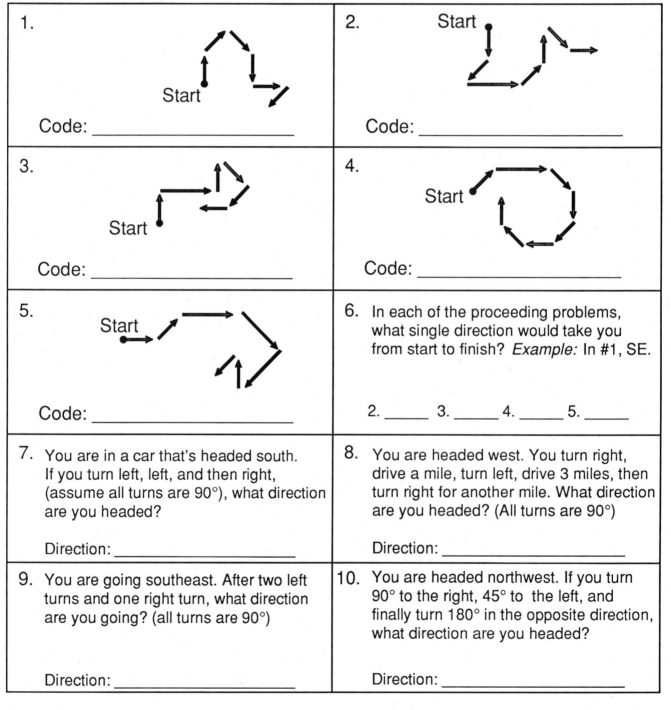

1.

Start

Code: _____

2.

Start

Code: _____

3.

Start

Code: _____

4.

Start

Code: _____

5.

Start

Code: _____

6. In each of the proceeding problems, what single direction would take you from start to finish? *Example:* In #1, SE.

2. _____   3. _____   4. _____   5. _____

7. You are in a car that's headed south. If you turn left, left, and then right, (assume all turns are 90°), what direction are you headed?

Direction: _____

8. You are headed west. You turn right, drive a mile, turn left, drive 3 miles, then turn right for another mile. What direction are you headed? (All turns are 90°)

Direction: _____

9. You are going southeast. After two left turns and one right turn, what direction are you going? (all turns are 90°)

Direction: _____

10. You are headed northwest. If you turn 90° to the right, 45° to the left, and finally turn 180° in the opposite direction, what direction are you headed?

Direction: _____

REFLECT ON THESE WORDS

Each phrase or sentence below has been reflected horizontally or vertically. Decode each saying and write it on the line.

LOOK BEFORE YOU LEAP.

_____

All for one, one for all.

_____

Absence makes the heart grow fonder.

_____

A stitch in times saves nine.

_____

Early to bed, early to rise ...

... I have a dream ...

_____   _____

I regret that I have but one life to give to my country.

_____

Smile and the world smiles with you.

_____

Big frog in a little pond.

_____

Reading backwards is not difficult.

_____

MATCHING SHAPES

◆

1. Which two figures below are exactly the same?
   Draw a ring around their letters.

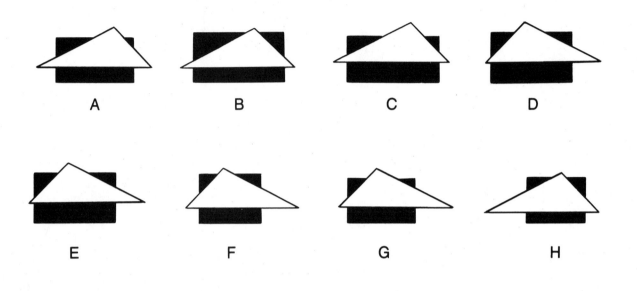

A   B   C   D

E   F   G   H

---

2. Match each numbered shape with its congruent
   lettered shape.

1. _____   2. _____   3. _____   4. _____   5. _____   6. _____

7. _____   8. _____   9. _____   10. _____   11. _____

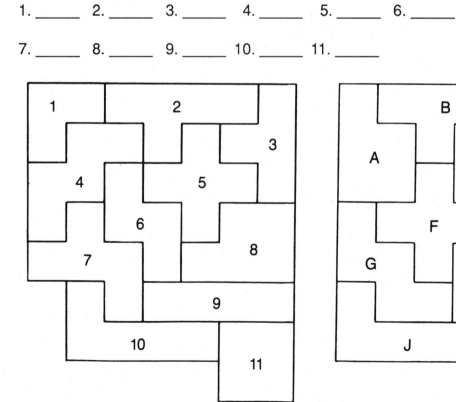

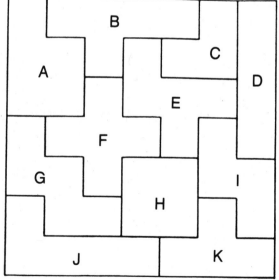

CRITICAL THINKING ACTIVITIES IN PATTERNS, IMAGERY, LOGIC (Secondary)
© Dale Seymour Publications

MIRROR IMAGES (I)

◆

1. Which figures below have horizontal lines of symmetry? _____

2. Which figures below have vertical lines of symmetry?_____

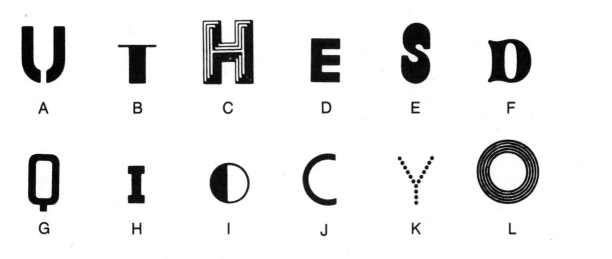

3. Which dominoes have horizontal lines of symmetry? _____

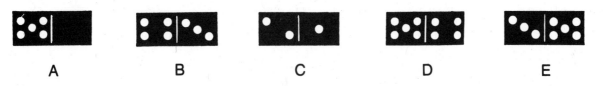

4. Complete these drawings. Make them symmetrical.

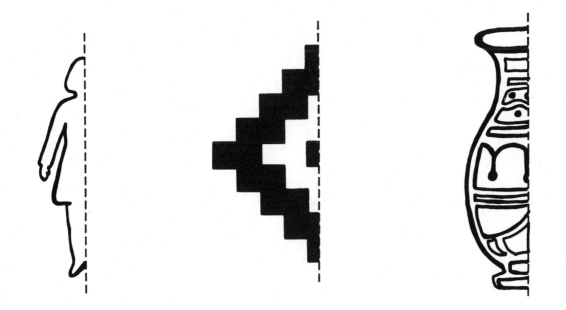

DOT DESIGNS (I)

Copy each design on the blank grid.

1.

2.   3.   4.

ROTATING GEARS ◆

Indicate whether the gears below will turn clockwise (CW) or counterclockwise (CCW).

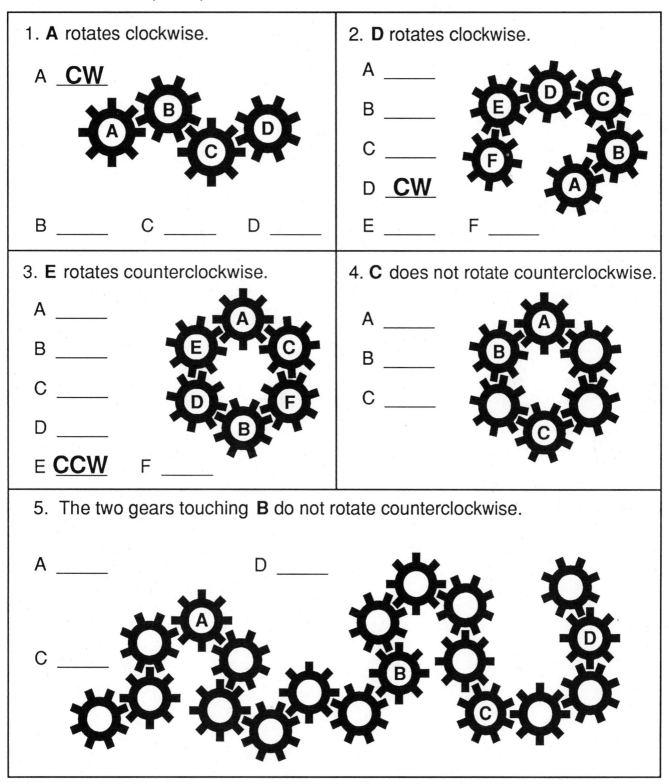

1. **A** rotates clockwise.

A **CW**

B _____   C _____   D _____

2. **D** rotates clockwise.

A _____

B _____

C _____

D **CW**

E _____   F _____

3. **E** rotates counterclockwise.

A _____

B _____

C _____

D _____

E **CCW**   F _____

4. **C** does not rotate counterclockwise.

A _____

B _____

C _____

5. The two gears touching **B** do not rotate counterclockwise.

A _____   D _____

C _____

STARS IN YOUR EYES

◆

Follow the steps below to draw an interesting design that looks three-dimensional.

1. On a sheet of 1/8-inch graph paper, draw a vertical axis about one inch from the left and a horizontal axis about two inches from the bottom. Number the squares along each axis by 5's, from 1 to 50.

Do steps 2–8 in pencil:

2. Plot and label points A(26,44), B(45,32), C(42,9), D(19,6) and E(8,27).

3. Draw $\overline{AB}$, $\overline{BC}$, $\overline{CD}$, $\overline{DE}$, and $\overline{EA}$.

4. Draw $\overline{AD}$, $\overline{AC}$, $\overline{BE}$, $\overline{BD}$, and $\overline{CE}$.

5. Label points F (intersection of $\overline{AD}$ and $\overline{EB}$), G (intersection of $\overline{AC}$ and $\overline{BE}$), H (intersection of $\overline{BD}$ and $\overline{AC}$), I (intersection of $\overline{CE}$ and $\overline{BD}$), and J (intersection of $\overline{CE}$ and $\overline{AD}$).

6. Plot and label point M (32,24).

7. Erase line segments $\overline{FG}$, $\overline{GH}$, $\overline{HI}$, $\overline{IJ}$, and $\overline{JF}$.

8. Draw line segments $\overline{MA}$, $\overline{MG}$, $\overline{MB}$, $\overline{MH}$, $\overline{MC}$, $\overline{MI}$, $\overline{MD}$, $\overline{MJ}$, $\overline{ME}$, and $\overline{MF}$.

9. Draw all existing line segments neatly in permanent ink. Let each line dry so that it won't smear.

10. Erase all remaining pencil marks.

11. For added effect, color all triangles in each plane the same color.

CRITICAL THINKING ACTIVITIES IN PATTERNS, IMAGERY, LOGIC (Secondary)

SCALE DRAWINGS

◆

Draw accurate scale drawings of the objects given below, using a scale of 1 centimeter to 1 meter. Label your drawings. Use a ruler and a separate piece of paper.

Example: A door: 1 m by 2.5 m

2.5 m   1 cm = 1 m

1 m

1. A door: 0.8m by 2.3m

2. A window: 1m by 1.2m

3. A rectangular patio: 4.5m by 6m

4. Outline of a rectangular swimming pool: 8m by 15m

5. A desktop: 1.75m by 1.1m

6. A picture frame: 0.35m by 0.75m

7. A book: 0.15m by 0.23m

8. A tennis court: 6m by 11.5m

9. A gameboard: 0.5m by 0.5m

10. A sheet of paper: 0.25m by 0.45m

WHERE HAVE ALL THE POLYGONS GONE?   ◆

Count the number of polygons asked for in the figure below.
Be careful— many of them overlap.

Count the number of polygons asked for in the figure below.
Be careful—many overlap.

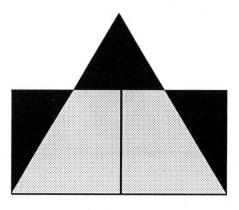

1. How many squares? ___	2. How many triangles? ___
3. How many equilateral triangles? ___	4. How many rectangles? ___
5. How many right triangles? ___	6. How many quadrilaterals? ___
7. How many pentagons? ___	8. How many regular polygons? ___

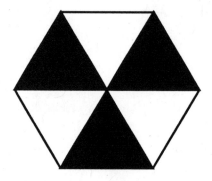

Answer questions 9–12 about the figure above.

9. How many triangles? ___	10. How many parallelograms? ___
11. How many trapezoids? ___	12. How many hexagons? ___

CRITICAL THINKING ACTIVITIES IN PATTERNS, IMAGERY, LOGIC (Secondary)
© Dale Seymour Publications

MAP MATH

Study the map below. In each problem, imagine that you are in a car looking ahead at the road sign. Use the circled letters to indicate a map location.

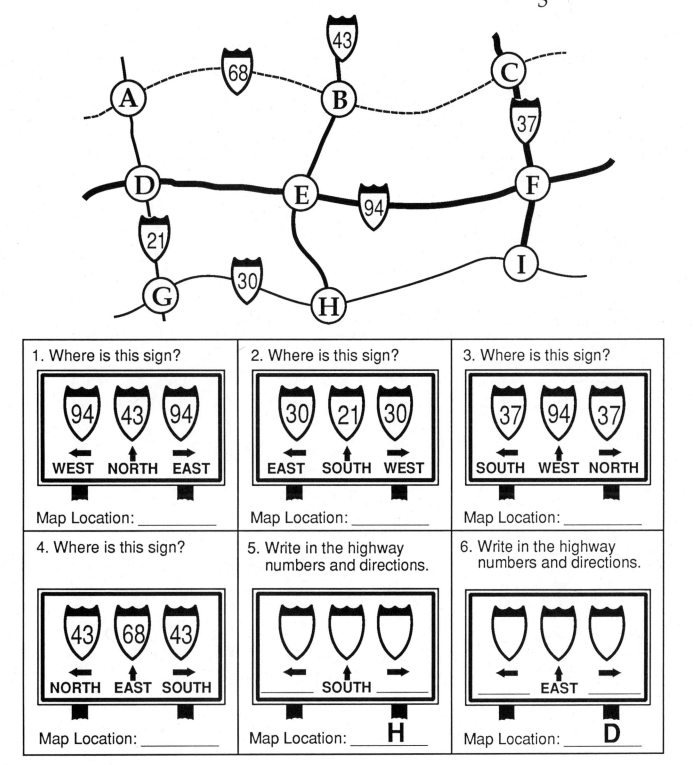

1. Where is this sign?

94	43	94
←	↑	→
WEST	NORTH	EAST

Map Location: _____

2. Where is this sign?

30	21	30
←	↑	→
EAST	SOUTH	WEST

Map Location: _____

3. Where is this sign?

37	94	37
←	↑	→
SOUTH	WEST	NORTH

Map Location: _____

4. Where is this sign?

43	68	43
←	↑	→
NORTH	EAST	SOUTH

Map Location: _____

5. Write in the highway numbers and directions.

←	↑	→
_____	SOUTH	_____

Map Location: **H**

6. Write in the highway numbers and directions.

←	↑	→
_____	EAST	_____

Map Location: **D**

CONFOUNDING SPIRAL

◆

Cut out the squares. Fit them together to make a
spiral with a white circle in the center.

CRITICAL THINKING ACTIVITIES IN PATTERNS, IMAGERY, LOGIC (Secondary)

LETTER PUZZLE (II)

◆◆

Compare the puzzle pieces with the lettered ones in the puzzle.
Write the correct letter on each piece.

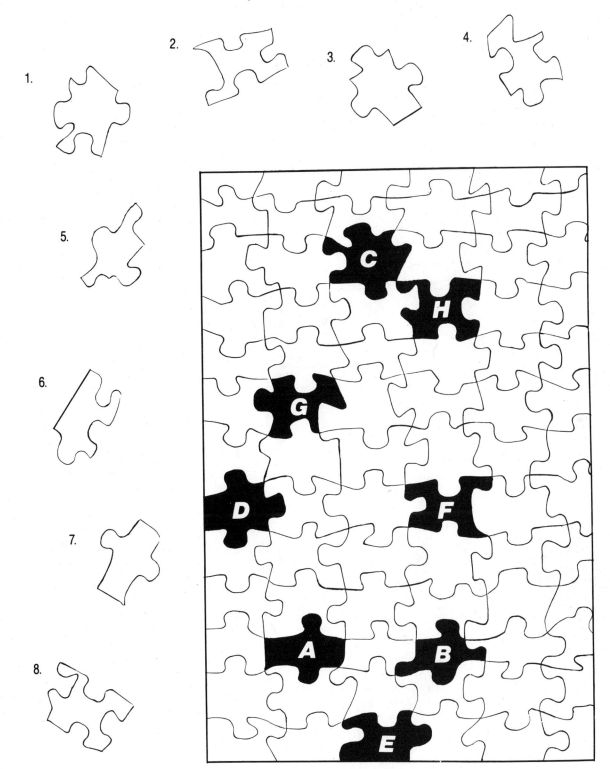

OVERLAPPING PANELS

Circular panels A–F below are transparent.

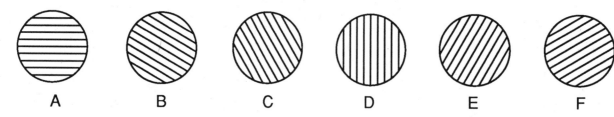

A   B   C   D   E   F

The figures in 1–7 were created by overlapping two or more of the six panels. List which of the six panels were used to create the numbered figure.

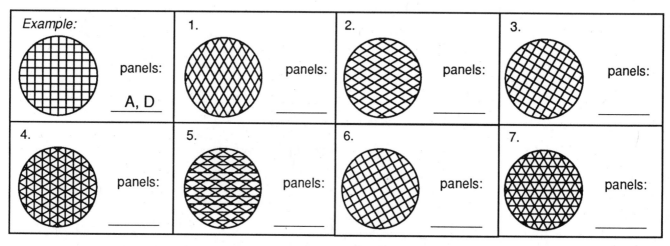

Example:	panels: A, D	1. panels: ___	2. panels: ___	3. panels: ___
4. panels: ___		5. panels: ___	6. panels: ___	7. panels: ___

Panel X was reflected (flipped) to form Panel Y. The designs below were created by rotating Panels X and Y and placing one over the other, or one over itself. Identify the four pairs of bottom edges in each problem.

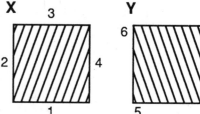

Example:
```
    3   7
6
2       4
        8
  5   1
```
__1__ and __5__ (and so on)

8. ___ and ___ ___ and ___
   ___ and ___ ___ and ___

9. ___ and ___ ___ and ___
   ___ and ___ ___ and ___

10. ___ and ___ ___ and ___
    ___ and ___ ___ and ___

11. ___ and ___ ___ and ___
    ___ and ___ ___ and ___

12. ___ and ___ ___ and ___
    ___ and ___ ___ and ___

13. ___ and ___ ___ and ___
    ___ and ___ ___ and ___

14. ___ and ___ ___ and ___
    ___ and ___ ___ and ___

CRITICAL THINKING ACTIVITIES IN PATTERNS, IMAGERY, LOGIC (Secondary)

WHICH WAY SUBWAY?

◆◆

Choose the diagram and the direction that fit the story.

Example: You are walking east. You turn left down an escalator. You step on the platform. You board the train on your right. You turn right in the direction the train is traveling. Which diagram matches the story?

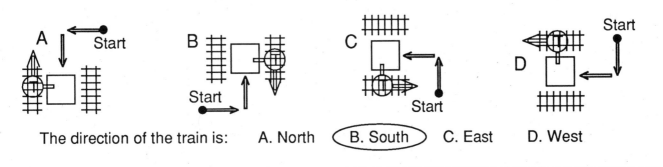

The direction of the train is: A. North   ⟨ B. South ⟩   C. East   D. West

Use the following diagrams for solving problems 1 to 4. Write **N, S, E** or **W** for the direction the train is headed.

A Start	B Start	C Start	D Start
E Start	F Start	G Start	F Start

1. You are walking north. Turn right. Turn right down the escalator. Step on the platform. Board the train on your left and turn right to travel forward.

    Diagram _____   Direction _____

2. You are walking east. Turn left into a tunnel, then right down an escalator. You step on the platform, take the train on your left, and travel forward to the right.

    Diagram _____   Direction _____

3. You are walking south. You turn left down an escalator. You turn left at the base of the escalator and walk to the platform. You board the train on your left, then face right. The train travels forward.

    Diagram _____   Direction _____

4. You are walking west. Turn right into a tunnel. Turn right down an escalator. Step on the platform. Board the train on your left, then face left to travel forward.

    Diagram _____   Direction _____

REFLECT ON THIS

◆◆

When a shape is reflected across a line of reflection, think of it as being flipped over. When reflected, the object retains the same shape. Also, if a point is connected with its reflected point, the line connecting the two points will be perpendicular to the line of reflection. In the example shown below, a triangle is reflected across the dotted line of reflection.

Draw a reflection of each of the twelve shapes below. Reflect your drawing across the given dotted line of reflection.

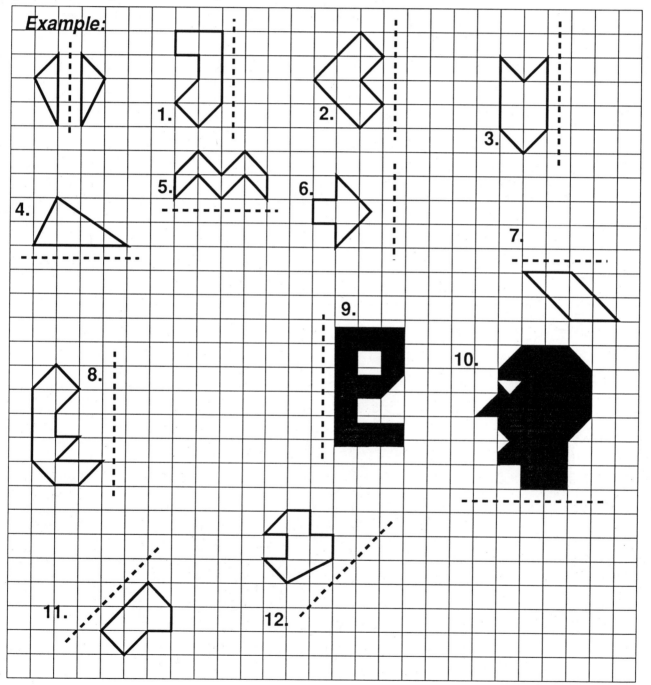

CRITICAL THINKING ACTIVITIES IN PATTERNS, IMAGERY, LOGIC (Secondary)
© Dale Seymour Publications

CRAZY CONGRUENT SHAPES

◆◆

1. Which two shapes are congruent? Draw a ring around the two correct shapes.

2. If possible, match each numbered shape with its congruent lettered shape. Write the correct letter next to the number.

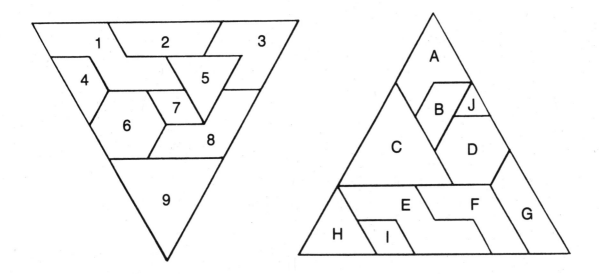

3. Match each numbered shape with its congruent lettered shape. Write the correct letter next to the number. Some shapes may be flipped.

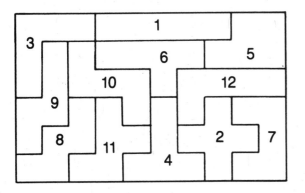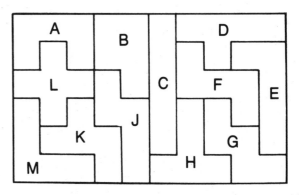

MIRROR IMAGES (II)

1. Which figures have no line of symmetry? Draw a ring around the letter of each one.

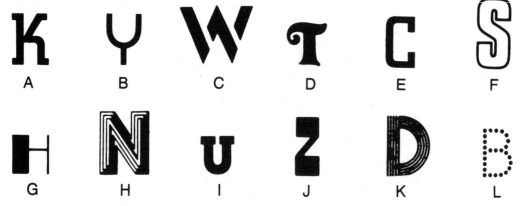

2. If you rotate something 180° and it is identical to its original position, it has *rotational symmetry.* Turn this page 180°. Do any of the letters above have rotational symmetry? If so, which letters? _____

3. Which pairs of dominoes below have vertical lines of symmetry? _____

4. Which have horizontal lines of symmetry? _____

5. Which have rotational symmetry? _____

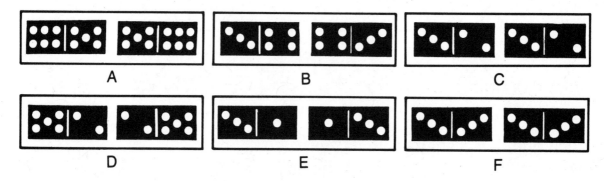

6. Complete these drawings. Make them symmetrical.

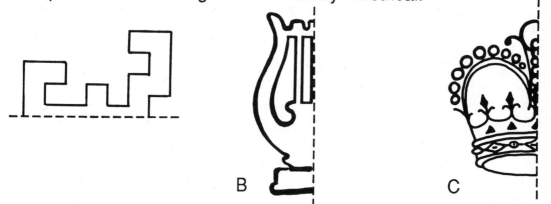

CRITICAL THINKING ACTIVITIES IN PATTERNS, IMAGERY, LOGIC (Secondary)

SYMMETRICAL IMAGES

◆◆

Draw all lines of symmetry on each figure. If there are none, write "none."

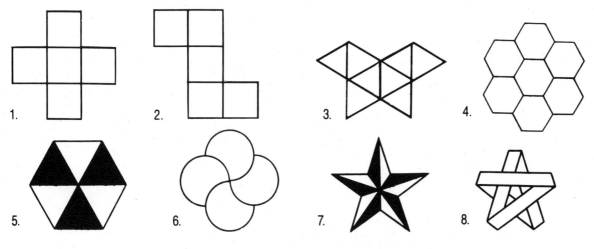

1.

2.

3.

4.

5.

6.

7.

8.

Copy each figure on the grid. Does either figure contain symmetry? If so, which one? _____

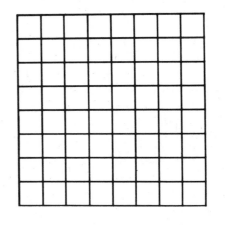

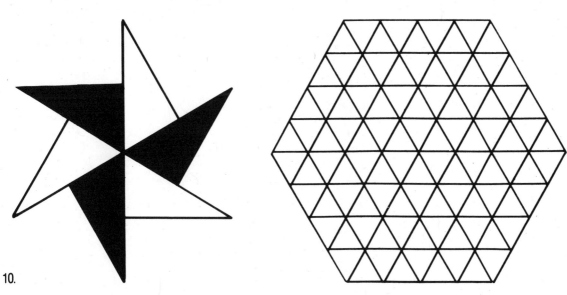

9.

10.

DOT DESIGNS (II)

Copy each design on the blank grid below it.

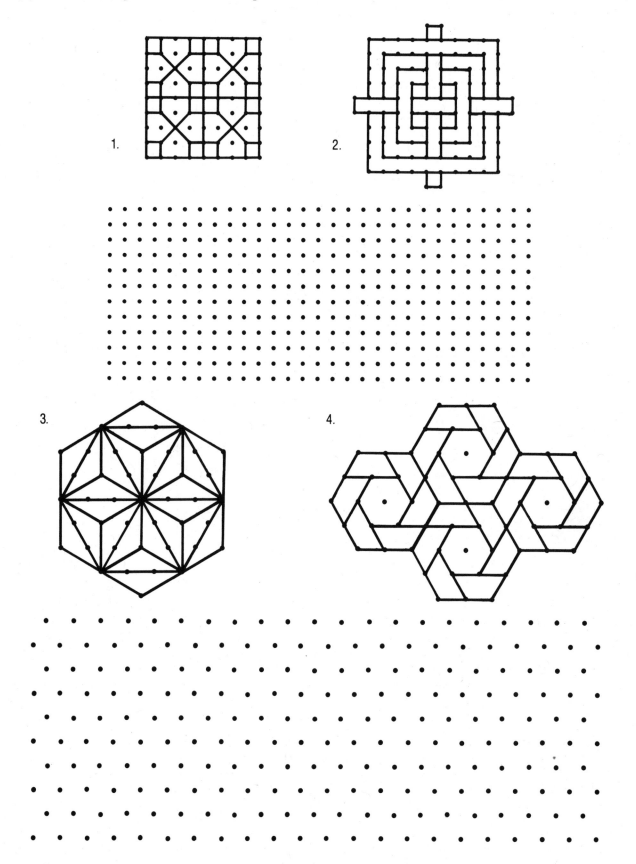

1.

2.

3.

4.

CRITICAL THINKING ACTIVITIES IN PATTERNS, IMAGERY, LOGIC (Secondary)
© Dale Seymour Publications

TREASURE IN THE PARK

You find a note that gives the secret location of a hidden sack of money in the local park. The note says, "The treasure is located at a point 75 feet from the flag pole, 55 feet from the fountain, and 60 feet from the midpoint of a straight line between the two big trees."

Use a compass and straightedge on the diagram below to find the location of the treasure.

List the treasure's grid location: _____

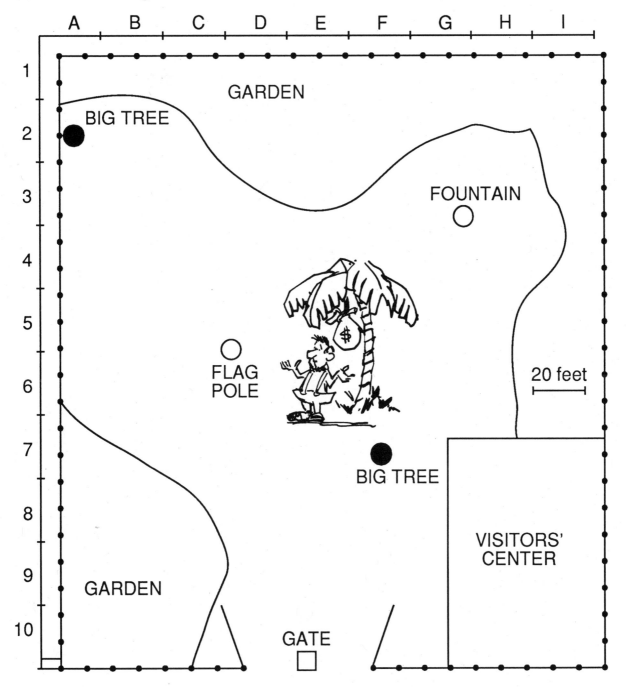

TRIANGLE TRIUMPH

◆◆

1. Draw all three angle bisectors of each triangle.

2. Draw all three medians of each triangle. (A median joins a vertex to the midpoint of the opposite side.)

3. Draw all three perpendicular bisectors of the sides of each triangle.

4. Draw all three altitudes of each triangle.

In each case, the three segments you have drawn, or their extensions, should meet at a common point.

CRITICAL THINKING ACTIVITIES IN PATTERNS, IMAGERY, LOGIC (Secondary)
© Dale Seymour Publications

MATCHING CROSSES

◆◆

Shapes A, B, and C appear in the large grid below. Find the three and shade them in.

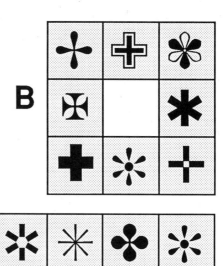

A

B

C

TANGLED TRIANGLES

◆◆

Count the number of triangles in each of the figures below.
Be careful—many of them overlap.

1. _____

2. _____

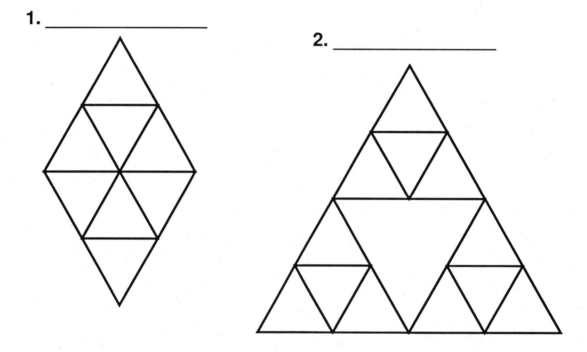

4. _____

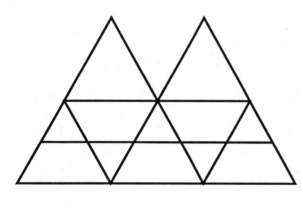

3. _____

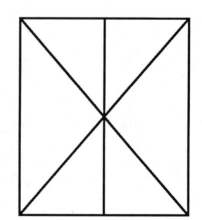

MAP ROUTES

◆◆

Study the map. In the problems below, draw a ring around every route that will *not* allow you to travel between the two points.

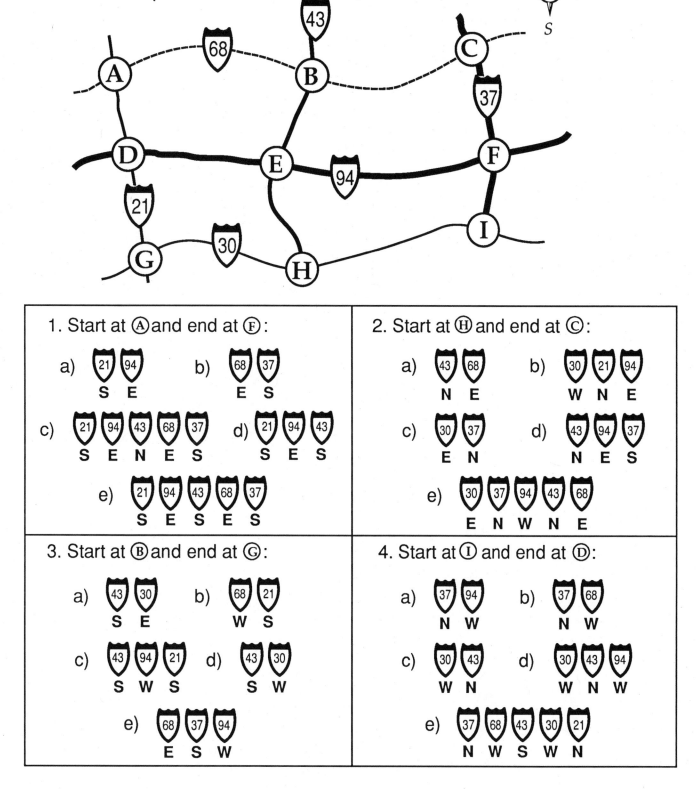

1. Start at Ⓐ and end at Ⓕ:

a) 21 94
   S E

b) 68 37
   E S

c) 21 94 43 68 37
   S E N E S

d) 21 94 43
   S E S

e) 21 94 43 68 37
   S E S E S

2. Start at Ⓗ and end at Ⓒ:

a) 43 68
   N E

b) 30 21 94
   W N E

c) 30 37
   E N

d) 43 94 37
   N E S

e) 30 37 94 43 68
   E N W N E

3. Start at Ⓑ and end at Ⓖ:

a) 43 30
   S E

b) 68 21
   W S

c) 43 94 21
   S W S

d) 43 30
   S W

e) 68 37 94
   E S W

4. Start at Ⓘ and end at Ⓓ:

a) 37 94
   N W

b) 37 68
   N W

c) 30 43
   W N

d) 30 43 94
   W N W

e) 37 68 43 30 21
   N W S W N

BAR-RAD RANCH

Imagine that a small box of gold coins is hidden on the Bar-Rad Ranch. Can you find its location? Here is the treasure map. Each number and letter refers to the space between the marks.

Clues: The treasure is 80 feet from the center of the well and 50 feet from the buried stake. The stake is equidistant from the southeast corner of the ranch house, the northwest corner of the bunk house, and the northeast corner of the corral fence. Use a compass and straightedge on the diagram below to find the two possible locations of the box of gold coins.

List the grid locations: _____

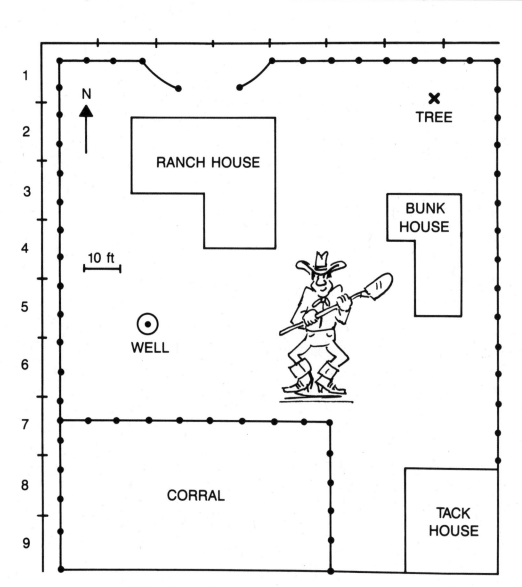

STAR LOCATIONS

◆◆

Each of the six designs in the squares below is a part of the
larger design under them. Use a number and letter to give the
location of each of the six sections of the drawing.

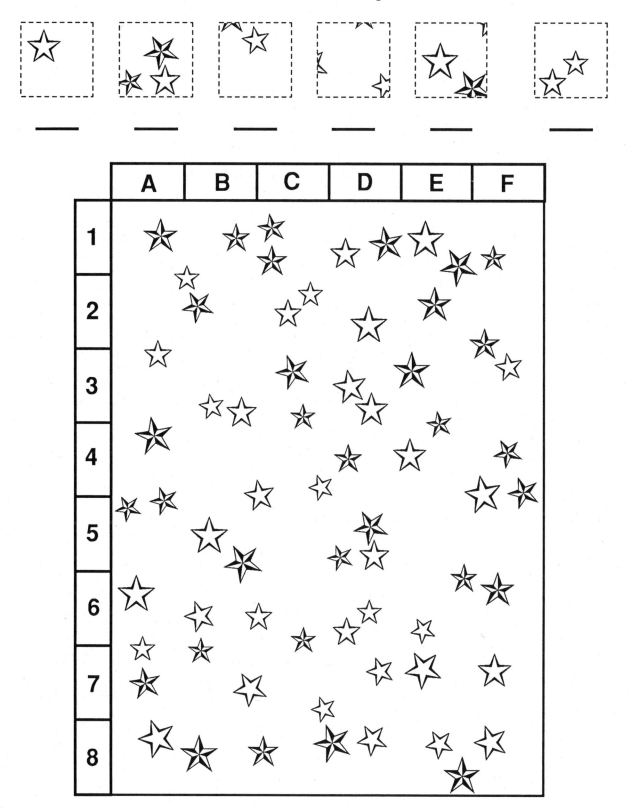

WEAVE PATTERN

Cut apart the puzzle pieces.
Put them together to make this design:

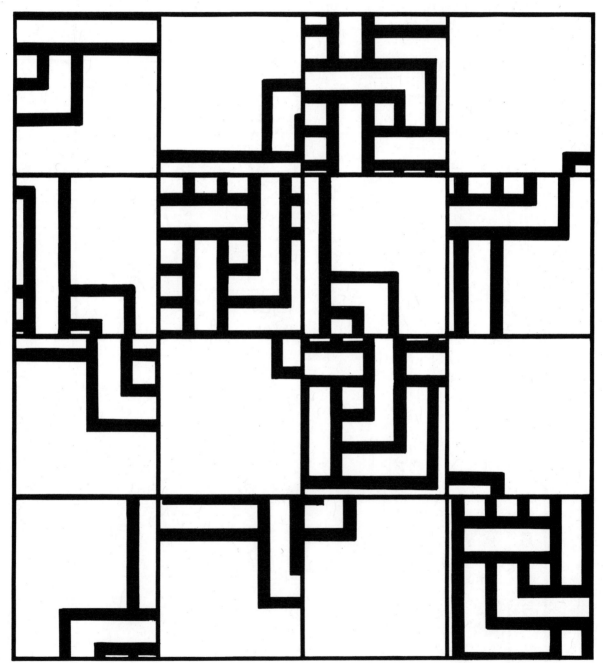

CRITICAL THINKING ACTIVITIES IN PATTERNS, IMAGERY, LOGIC (Secondary)

REPEATER SHAPES

When several *repeater shapes* are placed next to each
other, they form a similar but larger shape.

A square is a repeater shape, since four squares
produce a larger square.

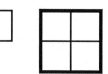

Decide if each shape below is a repeater shape.
Draw a figure showing the similar shape.
(Note: Some may not be possible.)

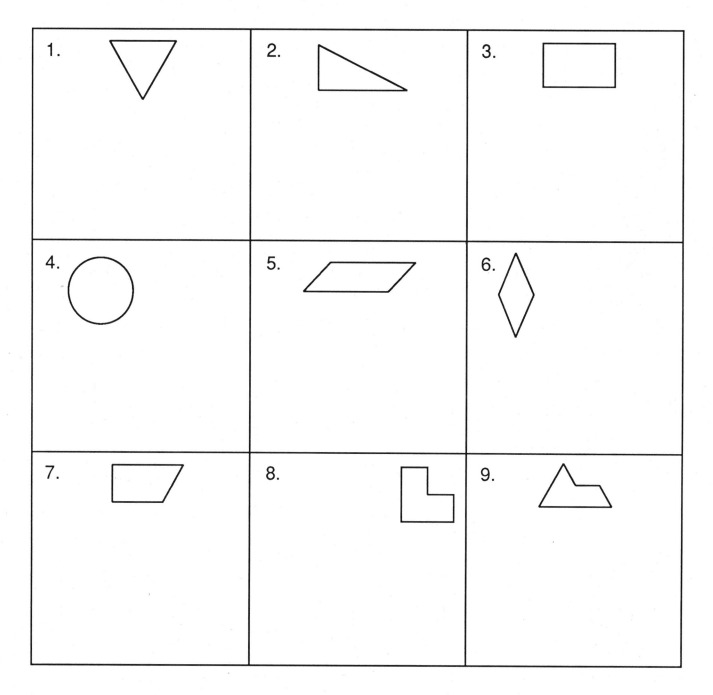

SHADE COVER

◆◆◆

Put a ring around the three figures in each problem that, when overlaid, will shade the entire figure with no duplicate shading.

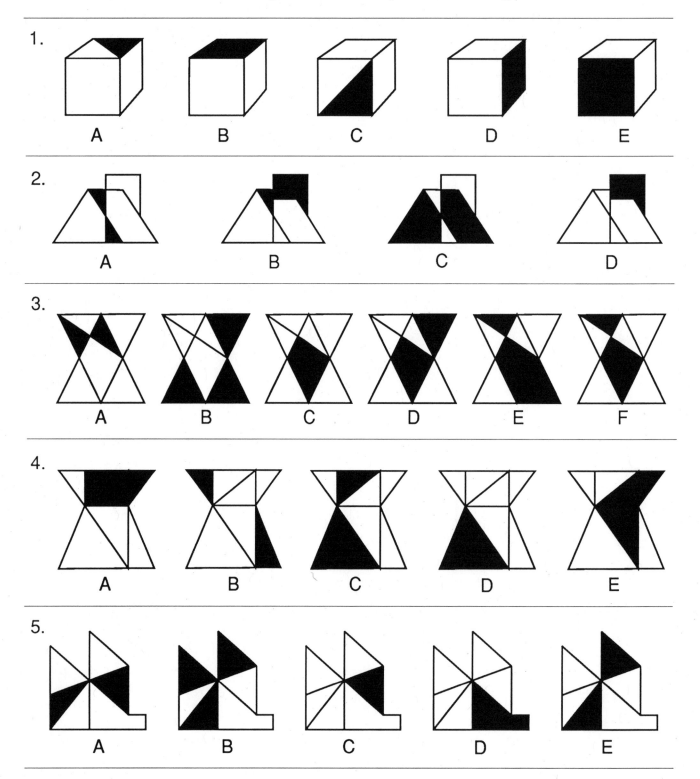

1.

A B C D E

2.

A B C D

3.

A B C D E F

4.

A B C D E

5.

A B C D E

CRITICAL THINKING ACTIVITIES IN PATTERNS, IMAGERY, LOGIC (Secondary)
© Dale Seymour Publications

FOLDING RECTANGLES

◆◆◆

Mentally fold each rectangle below along the dotted lines.
Then tell which pair of points in the rectangle will coincide.

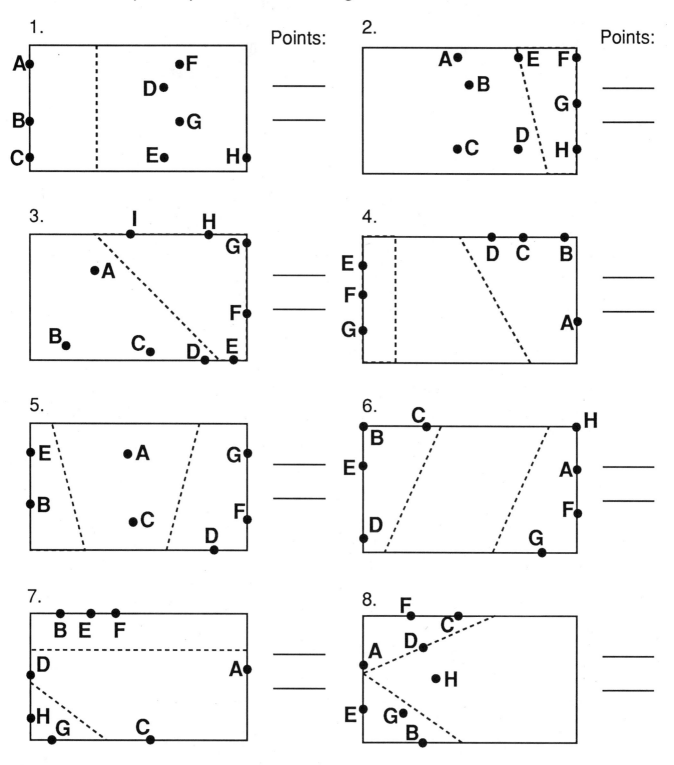

DIVIDE 'N CONGRUENT

◆◆◆

1. Divide each figure below into two congruent parts, if possible. If it is not possible, draw a ring around the number by the figure.

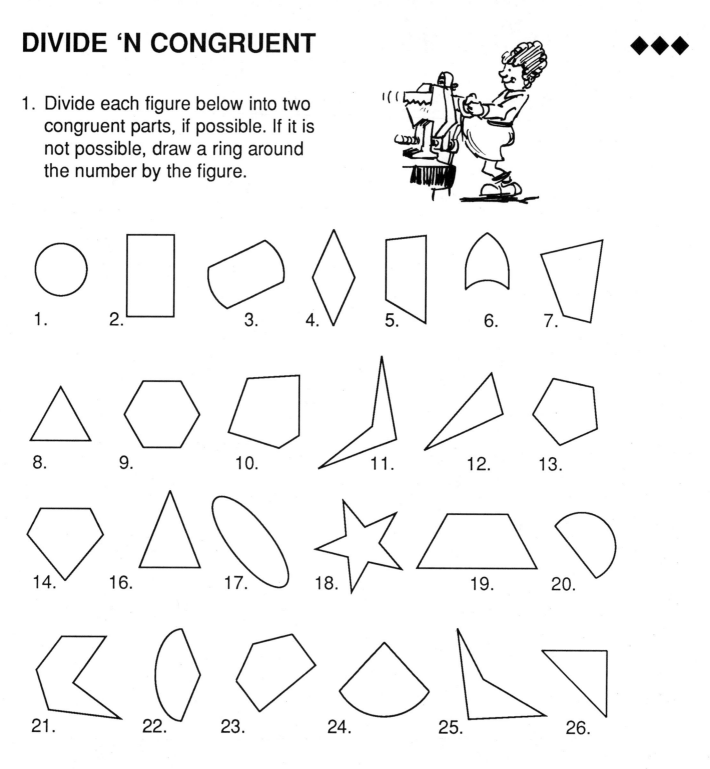

1.
2.
3.
4.
5.
6.
7.
8.
9.
10.
11.
12.
13.
14.
16.
17.
18.
19.
20.
21.
22.
23.
24.
25.
26.

2. Which figures can be divided into four congruent shapes?

_____

3. Which figures can be divided into three congruent shapes?

_____

CRITICAL THINKING ACTIVITIES IN PATTERNS, IMAGERY, LOGIC (Secondary)

DRAWING MIRROR IMAGES

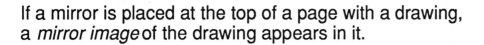

If a mirror is placed at the top of a page with a drawing,
a *mirror image* of the drawing appears in it.

Draw the mirror images of the drawings below.
Remember: the mirror is perpendicular to each drawing.

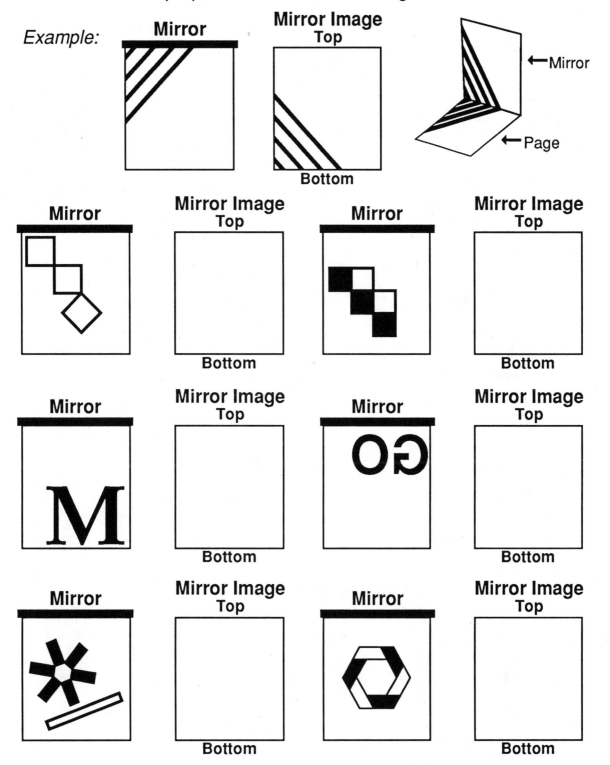

CRITICAL THINKING ACTIVITIES IN PATTERNS, IMAGERY, AND LOGIC (Secondary)

GRIDS AND SYMMETRY

Draw all lines of symmetry on each figure. If there are none, write "none."

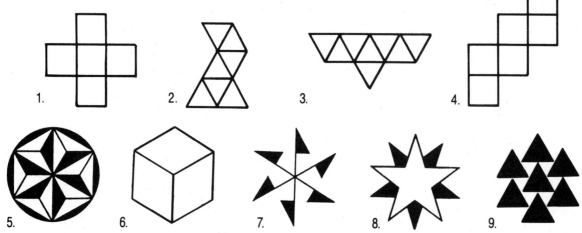

1.   2.   3.   4.

5.   6.   7.   8.   9.

Use a colored pencil or felt-tipped pen. Copy each figure on the blank grids. Does either figure have a line of symmetry? If so, which one? _____

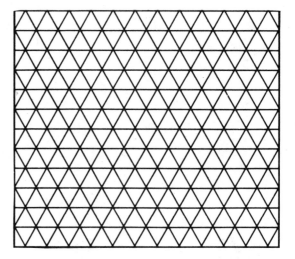

10.

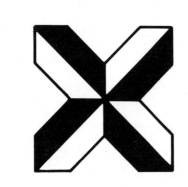

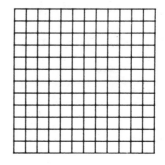

11.

CRITICAL THINKING ACTIVITIES IN PATTERNS, IMAGERY, LOGIC (Secondary)
© Dale Seymour Publications

IT'S YOUR TURN

Rotation can be either clockwise or counterclockwise—and around any point in the plane. The examples below show grey triangles rotated in a plane to the position of the white triangle.

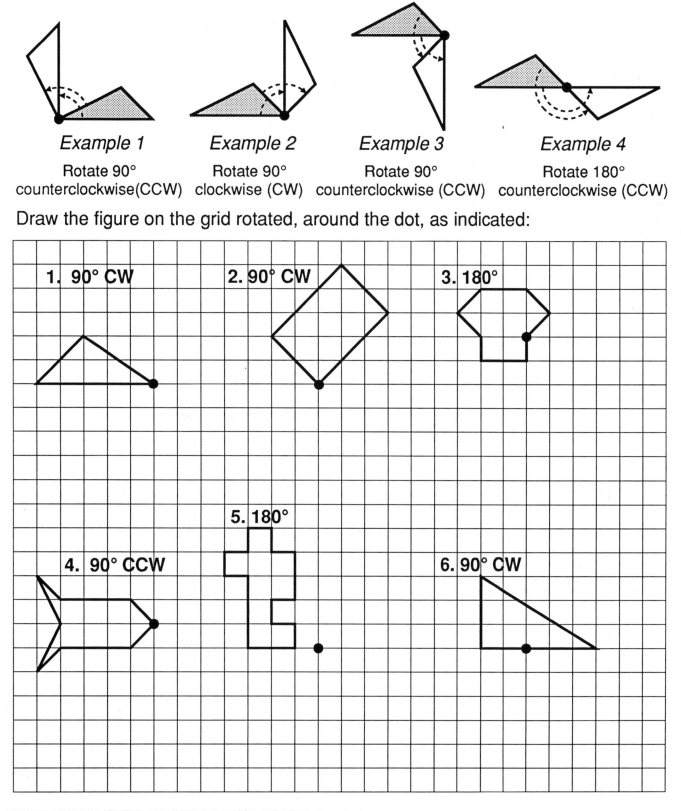

Example 1
Rotate 90°
counterclockwise(CCW)

Example 2
Rotate 90°
clockwise (CW)

Example 3
Rotate 90°
counterclockwise (CCW)

Example 4
Rotate 180°
counterclockwise (CCW)

Draw the figure on the grid rotated, around the dot, as indicated:

1. 90° CW

2. 90° CW

3. 180°

4. 90° CCW

5. 180°

6. 90° CW

CUBE FACES

◆◆◆

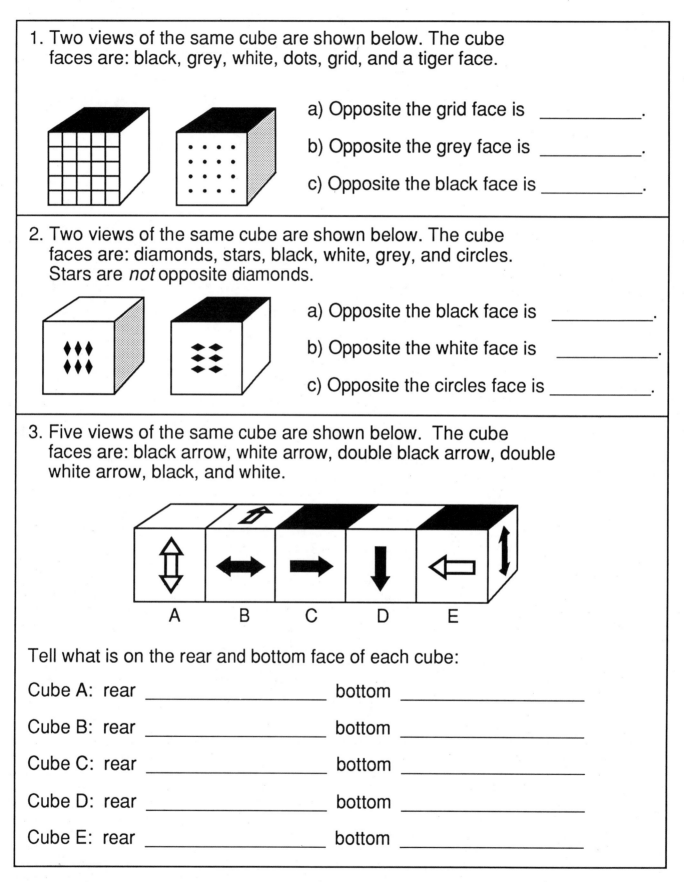

1. Two views of the same cube are shown below. The cube faces are: black, grey, white, dots, grid, and a tiger face.

   a) Opposite the grid face is _____.

   b) Opposite the grey face is _____.

   c) Opposite the black face is _____.

2. Two views of the same cube are shown below. The cube faces are: diamonds, stars, black, white, grey, and circles. Stars are *not* opposite diamonds.

   a) Opposite the black face is _____.

   b) Opposite the white face is _____.

   c) Opposite the circles face is _____.

3. Five views of the same cube are shown below. The cube faces are: black arrow, white arrow, double black arrow, double white arrow, black, and white.

   A   B   C   D   E

Tell what is on the rear and bottom face of each cube:

Cube A: rear _____ bottom _____

Cube B: rear _____ bottom _____

Cube C: rear _____ bottom _____

Cube D: rear _____ bottom _____

Cube E: rear _____ bottom _____

CRITICAL THINKING ACTIVITIES IN PATTERNS, IMAGERY, LOGIC (Secondary)
© Dale Seymour Publications

FIND THE SHAPES

Use these definitions:

> *Right triangle* — a triangle with one right angle.
> *Equilateral triangle* — a triangle with three equal
>   sides and three equal angles.
> *Isosceles triangle* — a triangle with two equal sides.

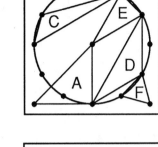

_____ 1. Write the letter of all right triangles in these
   drawings.

_____ 2. List all equilateral triangles.

_____ 3. List all isosceles triangles that aren't equilateral.

_____ 4. List all triangles that are none of the above.

Create different shapes below by connecting dots with
straight line segments:

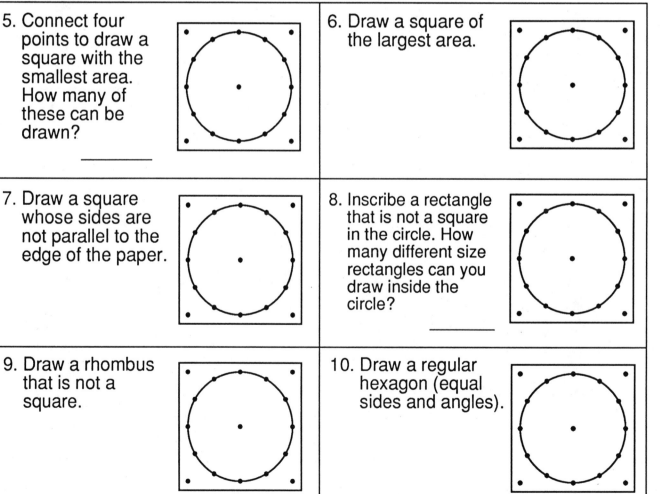

5. Connect four points to draw a square with the smallest area. How many of these can be drawn? _____	6. Draw a square of the largest area.
7. Draw a square whose sides are not parallel to the edge of the paper.	8. Inscribe a rectangle that is not a square in the circle. How many different size rectangles can you draw inside the circle? _____
9. Draw a rhombus that is not a square.	10. Draw a regular hexagon (equal sides and angles).

SEEING STARS

◆◆◆

Most of the star designs below occur only once in each row, column, and diagonal. However, *seven* of the stars occur twice:

- *Two* are in rows.
- *Two* are in columns.
- *Three* are in diagonals.

Find the seven repeating stars. Use letters and numbers to locate a position (for example, A1).

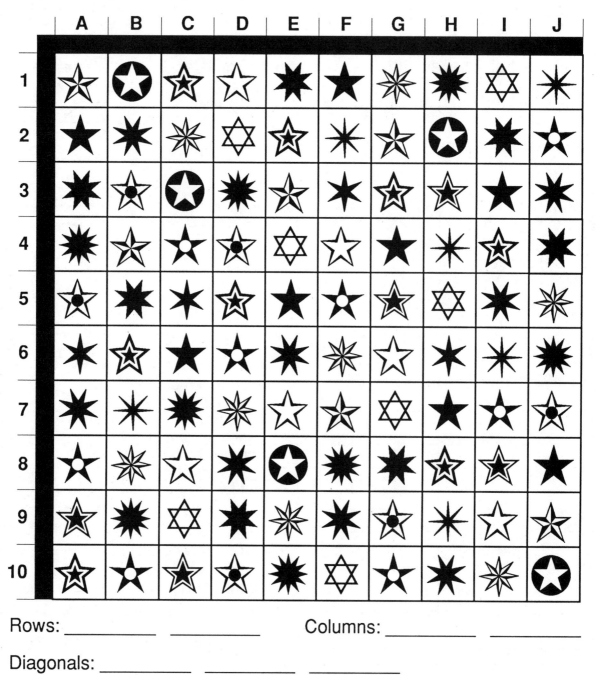

Rows: _____ _____   Columns: _____ _____

Diagonals: _____ _____ _____

CRITICAL THINKING ACTIVITIES IN PATTERNS, IMAGERY, LOGIC (Secondary)
© Dale Seymour Publications

CREATIVE DIVISIONS

◆◆◆

Divide each of these shapes into two congruent parts. Do it so that no two answers are the same. The small grid lines are helping lines. It is not necessary to draw on the grid lines.

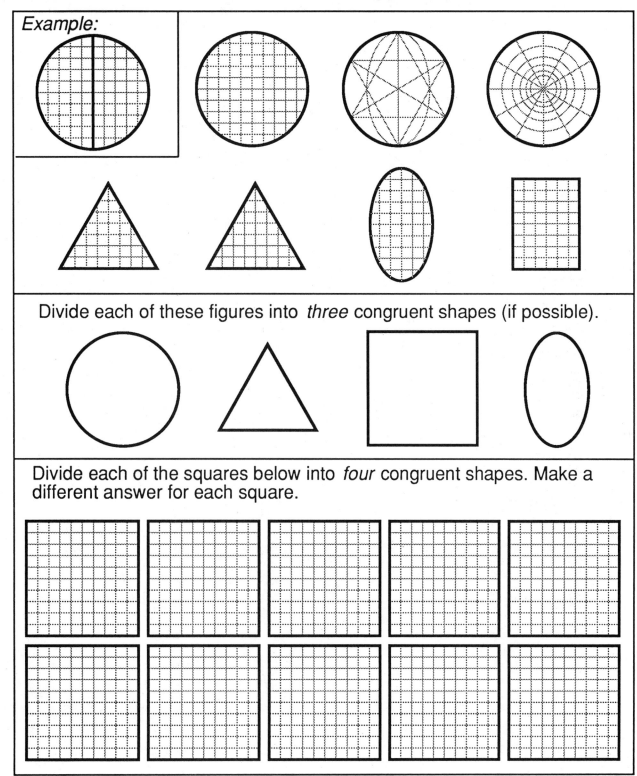

Divide each of these figures into *three* congruent shapes (if possible).

Divide each of the squares below into *four* congruent shapes. Make a different answer for each square.

CRITICAL THINKING ACTIVITIES IN PATTERNS, IMAGERY, AND LOGIC (Secondary)

© Dale Seymour Publications

MATCH POINTS

Visualize first folding point X to point Y,
then a second fold of point Z to point Y.
Draw a ring around the picture of the result.

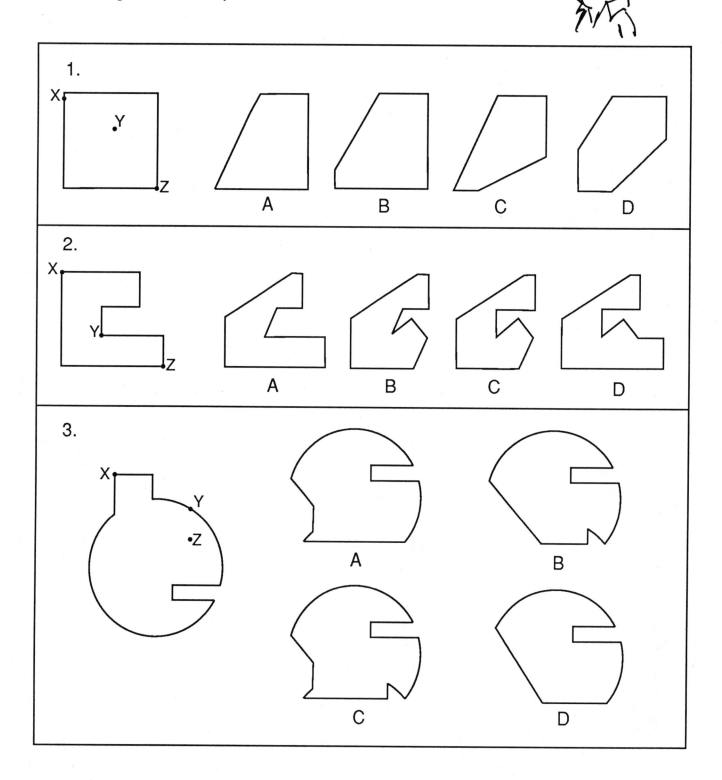

1.

A   B   C   D

2.

A   B   C   D

3.

A   B

C   D

CRITICAL THINKING ACTIVITIES IN PATTERNS, IMAGERY, LOGIC (Secondary)

CUBE VIEW

If the flat pattern on the left is folded, which cubes does it form? Draw a ring around the cubes made from the folded pattern in the four sections below.

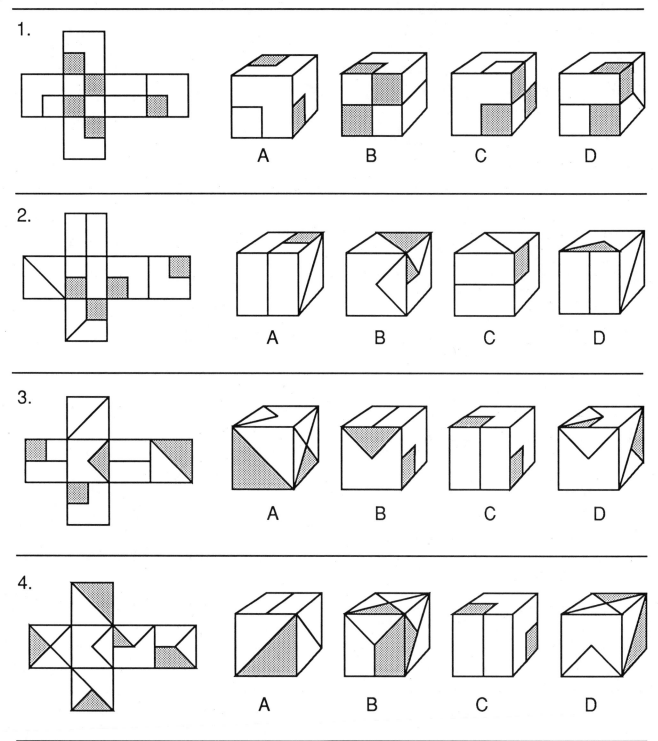

VISUALIZING INTERSECTIONS (I)

Draw a figure with the given number of intersections using all of the shapes listed in the "Shapes" column. Each shape must be involved in some intersection. If that's not possible, write "not possible." Study the examples in the first row.

Experiment with solutions on scratch paper first. When you are sure of an answer, then transfer it to this page.

Number of Intersecting Points

Shapes	1	2	3	4	5	6
Two triangles	◁◁	◁◁	◁◁	◁◁	✡	✡
Four line segments						
Two angles						
One angle One circle						
Two quadrilaterals						
Two circles						
One circle One square						

CRITICAL THINKING ACTIVITIES IN PATTERNS, IMAGERY, LOGIC (Secondary)
© Dale Seymour Publications

VISUALIZING INTERSECTIONS (II)

Draw a figure with the given number of intersections using all of the shapes listed in the "Shapes" column. Each shape must be involved in some intersection. If that's not possible, write "not possible." Study the examples in the first row.

Experiment with solutions on scratch paper first. When you are sure of an answer, then transfer it to this page.

Number of Intersecting Points

Shapes	1	2	3	4	5	6
Two triangles						
Two squares						
Two pentagons						
One circle One triangle						
Three triangles						
Three circles						
One circle One square One triangle						

REFLECTED ARROWS

◆◆◆

Ten different types of arrows appear below. For each type of arrow, nine pictures show the same arrow rotated to a new position, while one picture shows a reflected (flipped over) view of the arrow.

Draw a ring around the one arrow of each type that has been reflected.

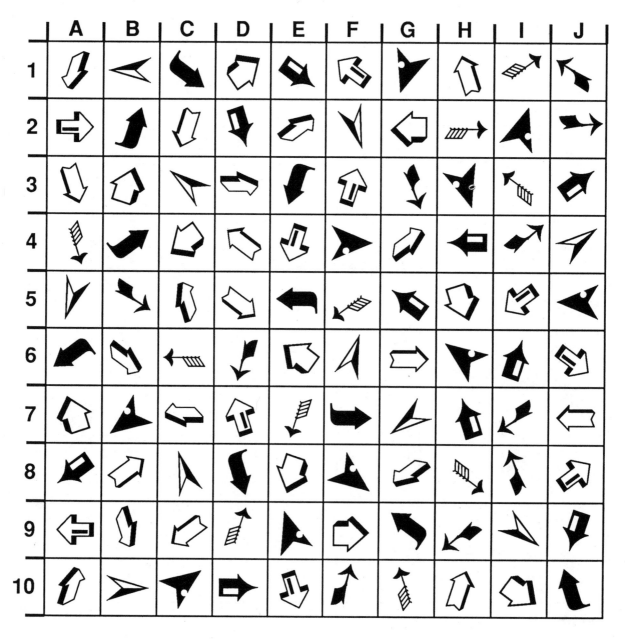

CRITICAL THINKING ACTIVITIES IN PATTERNS, IMAGERY, LOGIC (Secondary)
© Dale Seymour Publications

TANGLED RECTANGLES

Count all the rectangles, including squares, in each of the
figures below. Be careful—many of the rectangles overlap.
Hint: Try making an organized list of rectangles by size in
order to count them all.

1. _____

2. _____

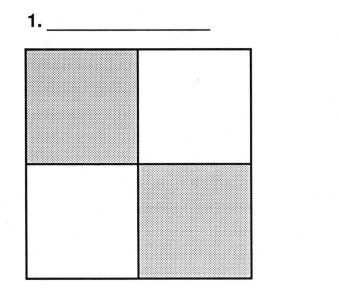

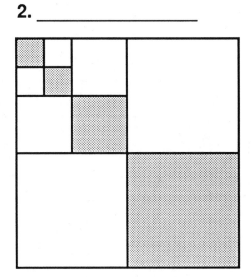

4. _____

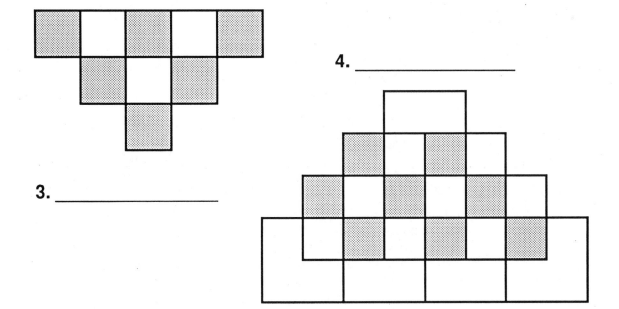

3. _____

DESIGN LOCATIONS

◆◆◆

Each of the six designs in the squares below is a part of the
larger design under them. Use a number and letter to give the
location of each of the six sections of the drawing.

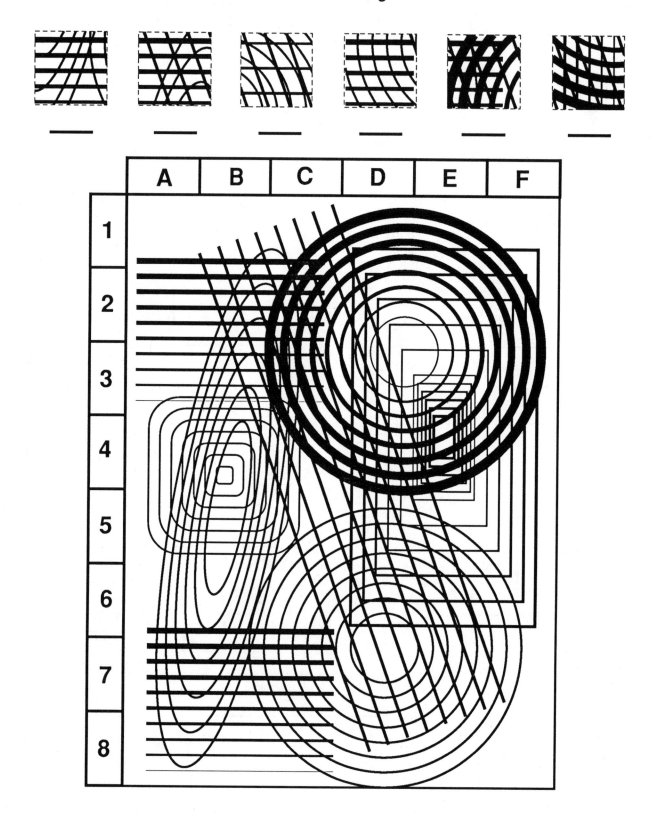

CRITICAL THINKING ACTIVITIES IN PATTERNS, IMAGERY, LOGIC (Secondary)
© Dale Seymour Publications

FOLD-A-FORM (I)

Each of the two-dimensional figures below can be folded into one of the solids on the right.

Draw a ring around the correct solid.

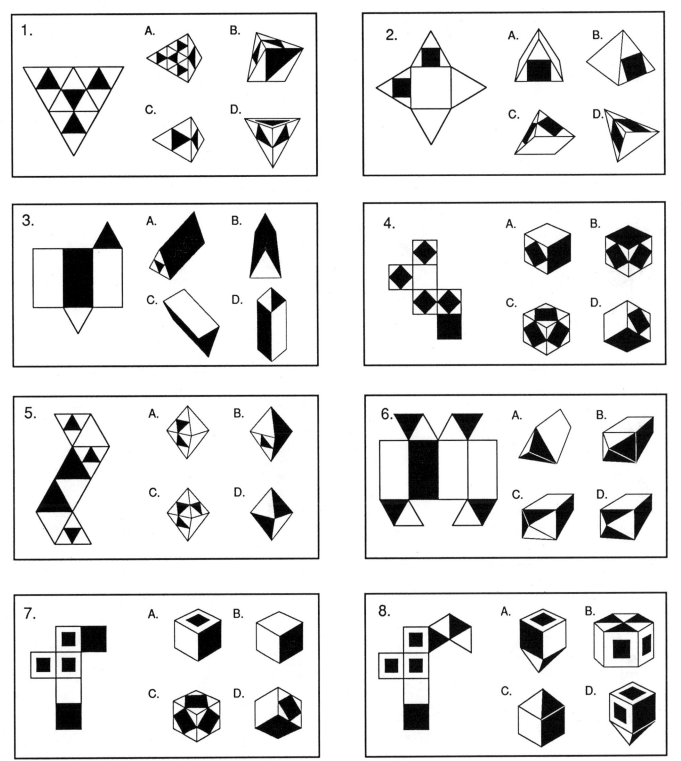

FOLD-A-FORM (II)

Each of the two-dimensional figures below can be folded into none, one, or more of the solids on the right.

Draw a ring around each correct solid.

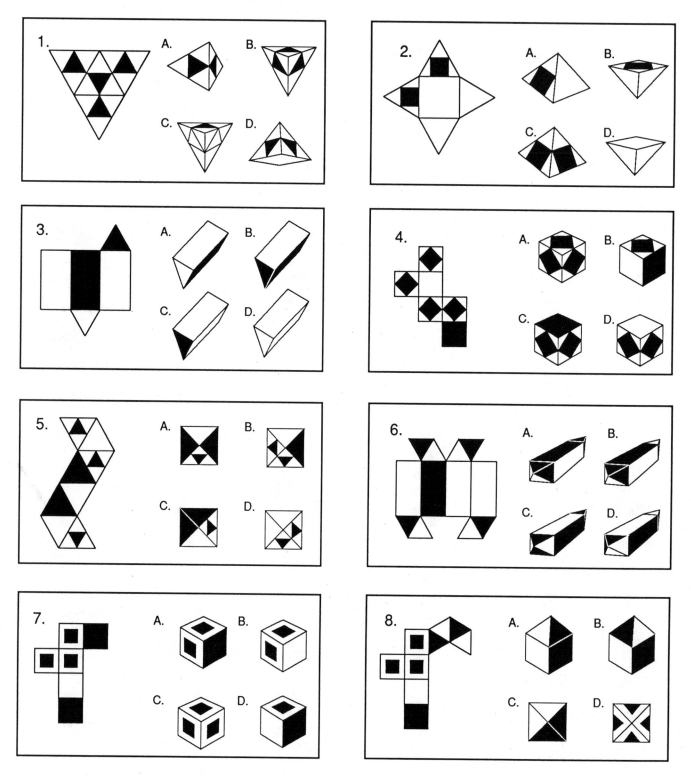

CRITICAL THINKING ACTIVITIES IN PATTERNS, IMAGERY, LOGIC (Secondary)
© Dale Seymour Publications

PERPLEXING PUZZLE

Cut apart the puzzle pieces.

Put them together to make this design:

CRITICAL THINKING ACTIVITIES IN PATTERNS, IMAGERY, LOGIC (Secondary)
© Dale Seymour Publications

PART 3: LOGIC

FIGURE SORT

◆

Write the number of each of the eight figures below in
the appropriate region of each diagram.

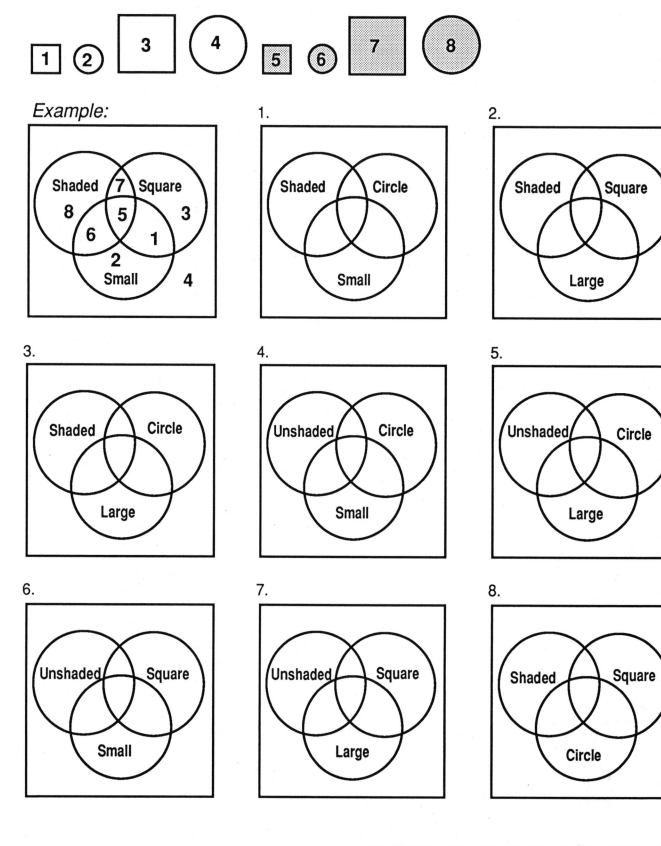

Example:

CRITICAL THINKING ACTIVITIES IN PATTERNS, IMAGERY, LOGIC (Secondary)
© Dale Seymour Publications

NUMBER JUGGLING (I)

Use any three of the four numbers 2, 3, 6, and 12 to make the
number sentences true. Use each number you select only once
in a problem.

1. $\bigcirc + \bigcirc + \bigcirc = 21$

2. $\bigcirc + \bigcirc - \bigcirc = 9$

3. $\bigcirc \times \bigcirc + \bigcirc = 20$

4. $\bigcirc \times \bigcirc - \bigcirc = 18$

5. $\bigcirc \times \bigcirc \times \bigcirc = 36$

6. $\bigcirc \times \bigcirc \div \bigcirc = 9$

7. $\bigcirc \times \bigcirc \div \bigcirc = 6$

8. $\bigcirc \div \bigcirc + \bigcirc = 5$

9. $\bigcirc \div \bigcirc - \bigcirc = 3$

10. $\bigcirc \div \bigcirc \div \bigcirc = 1$

11. $\bigcirc \div \bigcirc \div \bigcirc = 2$

12. $\bigcirc \times \bigcirc \div \bigcirc = 4$

LOGICAL FAMILIES

◆

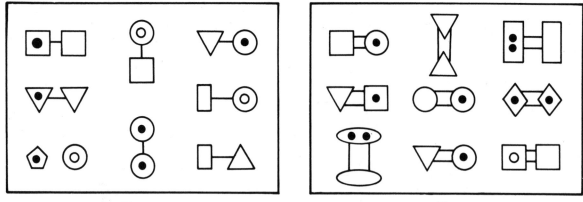

Nects   Tencs

1. Which of the following are Nects? Draw a ring around each correct letter.

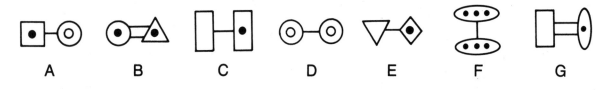

A   B   C   D   E   F   G

2. What is the distinguishing characteristic of a Tenc?

_____

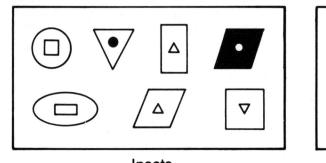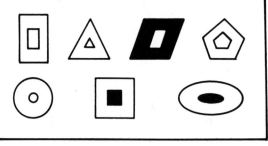

Insets   Setins

3. Which of the following are Setins? Draw a ring around each correct letter.

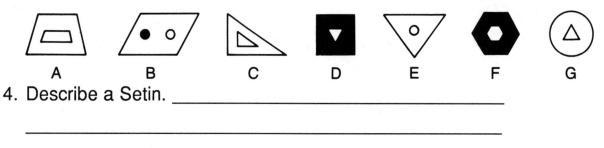

A   B   C   D   E   F   G

4. Describe a Setin. _____

_____

_____

CRITICAL THINKING ACTIVITIES IN PATTERNS, IMAGERY, LOGIC (Secondary)
© Dale Seymour Publications

COMPARING FACTS TO SOLVE PROBLEMS (I) ◆

1. Pat, Tiffany, and Joan are friends.
   Pat is taller than Joan.
   Joan is taller than Tiffany.
   Who is the shortest?

   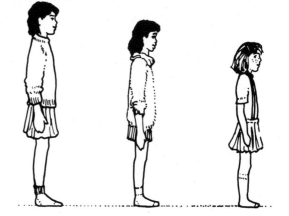

   _____

   _____

2. Cal has more money than Fred.
   Fred has less money than Don.
   Don has less money than Cal.

   Who has the least amount of money? _____

3. Harry is 2 years older than Jan.
   Mary is 1 year younger than Butch.
   Luis is 4 years older than Harry.
   Mary is 5 years older than Jan.

   How much older is Luis than Jan? _____

4. Three boys were comparing their house numbers. Each
   house number contains three digits. By coincidence, the
   sum of the digits of each house number is the same.
   a. None of the numbers contains a digit that is in one of the
      other numbers.
   b. None of the numbers begins with a 4.
   c. Bill's number is 252.
   d. Ben's number begins with a 6.
   e. Bart's number ends with a 1.

   What is Bart's house number? _____

INDUCTIVE REASONING

You use *inductive reasoning* if you reach a conclusion by making particular observations.

Example:

If a number is divisible by 4, is it divisible by 2?

   Examine some cases: 44, 60, 72, 36

Based on these cases, you should say, "Yes!" In fact, if the number is divisible by 4, then the ones digit is even (divisible by 2). Note: This is a conjecture only, not a proof!

For each statement below, examine five cases. Make a conjecture of "yes" or "no."

Yes/No

1. If a number is divisible by 2 and 5, is it divisible by 7? _____

2. If a number is divisible by 8, is it divisible by 4? _____

3. If a number is divisible by 10, is it divisible by 5? _____

4. If a number is divisible by 3, is it divisible by 9? _____

5. If a number is divisible by 2 and 4, is it divisible by 8? _____

6. If a number is divisible by 2 and 4, is it divisible by 6? _____

7. If a number is divisible by 2 and 8, is it divisible by 16? _____

8. If a number is divisible by 4 and 8, is it divisible by 12? _____

9. If a number is divisible by 3 and 4, is it divisible by 12? _____

10. If a number is divisible by 5 and 3, is it divisible by 15? _____

11. If a number is divisible by 9 and 2, is it divisible by 11? _____

12. If a number is divisible by 9 and 2, is it divisible by 18? _____

13. If a number is divisible by 2 and 7, is it divisible by 9? _____

14. If a number is divisible by 2 and 7, is it divisible by 14? _____

15. If a number is divisible by 3 and 6, is it divisible by 18? _____

CRITICAL THINKING ACTIVITIES IN PATTERNS, IMAGERY, LOGIC (Secondary)
© Dale Seymour Publications

NUMBER SEARCH

◆

Examples: List the numbers that are in both sets A and B.   18, 19, 25, 31, 40

List the numbers that are in set A only.   9, 12, 15, 17, 22, 30

1. List the numbers that are in both sets A and C. _____

2. List the numbers that are in both sets B and C. _____

3. List the numbers that are in set B only. _____

4. What is the sum of the numbers in set C only? _____

5. List the numbers that are in both sets A and B but not in set C. _____

6. What numbers are in set B but not in set A? _____

7. What is the sum of the numbers in all three sets, A, B, and C? _____

8. Which numbers are in set A but not in set C? _____

9. What is the sum of the numbers in set A only? _____

10. List the numbers that are in both sets B and C but not in set A. _____

FIND THE MISSING DIGITS (I)

Find the digits that will replace ★ and ¢ to make the problem correct.

1.
```
   ★5
   37
   51      ★ = _____
  +4¢      ¢ = _____
 ─────
  161
```

2.
```
  5,★18     ★ = _____
 −2,9¢6     ¢ = _____
 ──────
  2,772
```

3.
```
   ★8    ★ = _____
  +4★    ¢ = _____
 ─────
  1¢3
```

4.
```
   7★     ★ = _____
  × ¢     ¢ = _____
 ─────
  60¢
```

5.
```
      1★    ★ = _____
  ¢)133     ¢ = _____
```

6.
```
   2★
   47      ★ = _____
   ★1
  +8★      ¢ = _____
 ─────
  1¢4
```

7.
```
   ★3    ★ = _____
  × ¢    ¢ = _____
 ─────
  3¢1
```

8.
```
   ★¢    ★ = _____
  × 6    ¢ = _____
 ─────
  2¢★
```

CRITICAL THINKING ACTIVITIES IN PATTERNS, IMAGERY, LOGIC (Secondary)
© Dale Seymour Publications

SHAPE FAMILIES

◆

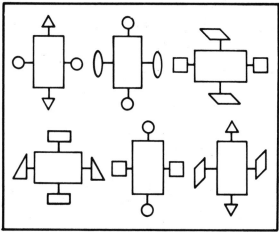

These are Sarms.

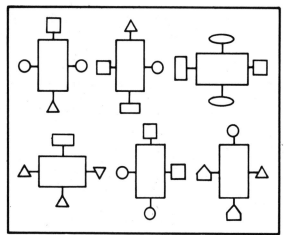

These are Darms.

1. Which of the following are Sarms? Draw a ring around each correct letter.

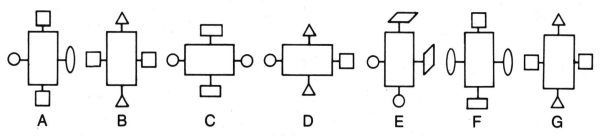

A   B   C   D   E   F   G

2. What is the difference between a Sarm and a Darm?

_____

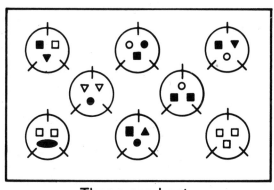

These are Lants.

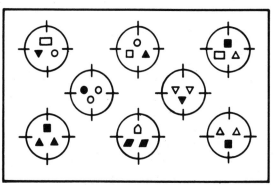

These are Jants.

3. Which of the following are Jants? Draw a ring around each correct letter.

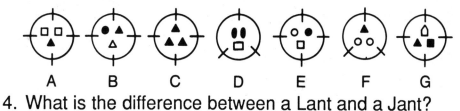

A   B   C   D   E   F   G

4. What is the difference between a Lant and a Jant?

_____

SOLVING WORD PROBLEMS WITH LOGIC (I) ◆

Draw a ring around each correct answer.

1. My number is a two-digit number.
   Your number is a one-digit number.
   Therefore, your number is less than my number.   true   false

2. Our numbers are both odd.
   Therefore, our numbers differ by 2.   true   false

3. My number has two digits.
   Your number is 5 less than mine.
   Therefore, my number is less than 5.   true   false

4. My number is greater than Fred's number.
   Your number is less than my number.
   Therefore, Fred's number could be greater than
   your number.   true   false

5. My number is less than 6.
   Your number is greater than 4.
   Therefore, our numbers couldn't be the same.   true   false

6. My number is 5. Your number is 7.
   Bill's number is 3 greater than mine.
   Therefore, Bill's number is 1 less than yours.   true   false

7. Your number is 1 greater than Sue's number.
   Sue's number is odd.
   My number is 3 less than Sue's number.
   Therefore, your number is even.   true   false

8. Your number is 3 greater than Phil's number.
   My number is 2 less than Phil's number.
   Therefore, my number is 5 greater than your number.   true   false

9. My number is 3 greater than Juan's number.
   Juan's number is 4 less than Ila's number.
   Ila's number is the same as Mary's.
   Therefore, Juan's number is 1 less than my number.   true   false

CRITICAL THINKING ACTIVITIES IN PATTERNS, IMAGERY, LOGIC (Secondary)

VENN DIAGRAMS

◆

Use the given information to place numbers in the Venn diagram. Answer the questions and write the numbers where they belong.

Set A represents even numbers less than 40.

Set B represents prime numbers less than 40.

Set C represents odd numbers less than 30.

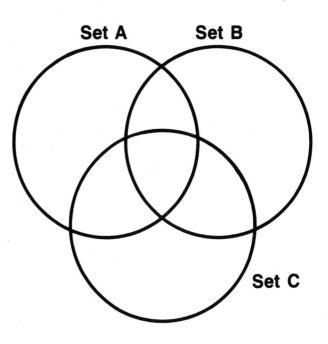

1. Where does 17 belong in this diagram? _____

_____

_____

2. Where does 36 belong in this diagram? _____

_____

3. The number 2 belongs to set _____ and set _____.

4. Where does 37 belong in this diagram? _____

_____

5. The number 28 belongs to set _____.

6. Where does 27 belong? _____

7. Where does 23 belong? _____

8. Where does 6 belong? _____

9. What is the least number that is a member of set A only? _____

10. What number belongs in the space that sets A, B, and C have in common?

_____

11. What is the greatest number that is an element of set B only?_____

12. What is the least number that belongs to both sets B and C? _____

ADDITION AND MULTIPLICATION LOGIC ◆

A, B, and C each stand for a different one-digit number. None
of the letters stands for zero.

$$\begin{array}{r} A \\ + \; B \\ \hline C \end{array}$$

1. If neither A nor B is odd, and C is not greater than

    7, then C is _____.

2. If B > 5 and A > 2, then C is _____.

3. If C < 5 and both A and B are odd, then A + B + C = _____.

4. If A and B are both divisible by 3, then C is _____.

5. If all three numbers are prime numbers, and C is more than 3

    times A, then B must be _____.

6. If one number is even and all three are prime numbers, then

    the two largest numbers differ by _____.

W, X, Y, and Z each stand for a different one-digit number.
None of the letters stands for zero.

$$\begin{array}{r} W \\ + \; X \\ \hline YZ \end{array}$$

1. Y is less than or equal to _____.

2. Since Z is not 0, then neither W nor X equals _____.

3. If X is less than 3, are Y and Z odd or even?

    Y is _____ and Z is _____.

4. If W, X, and Z are even and W + 4 = X, then

    W = _____, X = _____, Y = _____, and Z = _____.

5. If Y < Z and both W and X are odd, then Z = _____.

6. If W is a cubed number and X is a squared number,

    then Z is _____ and Y is either _____ or _____.

CRITICAL THINKING ACTIVITIES IN PATTERNS, IMAGERY, LOGIC (Secondary)
© Dale Seymour Publications

RADS, FADS, AND HADS

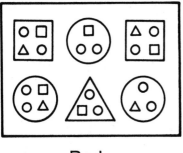

Rads

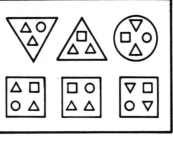

Fads

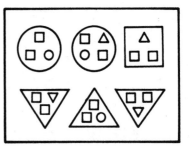

Hads

1. Which of the following are Hads?
   Draw a ring around each correct letter.

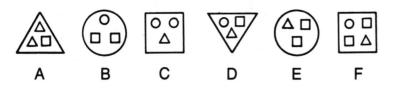

A   B   C   D   E   F

2. Which of the following are not Fads?
   Draw a ring around each correct letter.

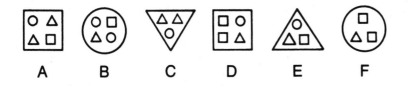

A   B   C   D   E   F

3. Which of the following are not Rads?
   Draw a ring around each correct letter.

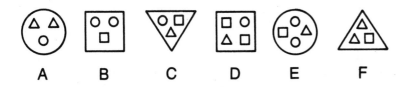

A   B   C   D   E   F

4. Draw a Fad.

LOGICAL STRATEGY

◆

Two people play the game of 5-in-a-row. Taking turns, one marks X's; the other marks O's. The first player to mark 5 in a row across, down, or diagonally wins. Answer the questions below each game. Identify the squares by column letters and row numbers.

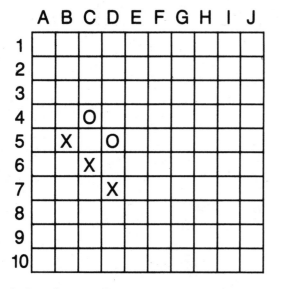

1. It is player O's turn next. What square should player O mark?

_____.

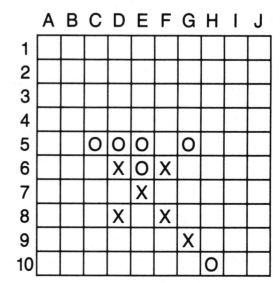

2. It is player X's turn next. What square should player X mark?

_____.

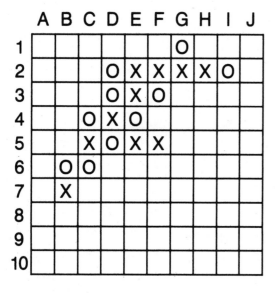

3. It is player O's turn next. What square will give player O a sure win? _____.

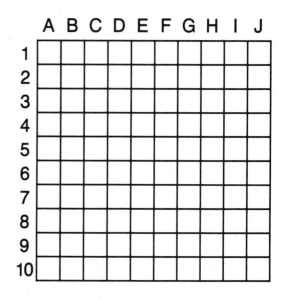

4. Use this grid to play 5-in-a-row with a friend.

CRITICAL THINKING ACTIVITIES IN PATTERNS, IMAGERY, LOGIC (Secondary)
© Dale Seymour Publications

CHANGING ATTRIBUTES (I)

◆

Begin with one of the figures below. Then change its attributes in sequence. (Change only one attribute at a time.)

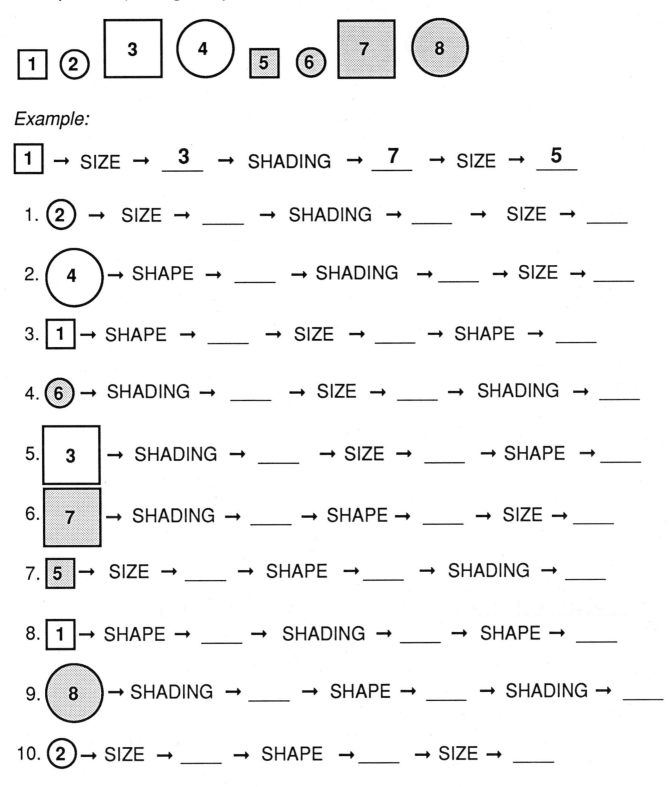

Example:

1 → SIZE → __3__ → SHADING → __7__ → SIZE → __5__

1. ② → SIZE → ____ → SHADING → ____ → SIZE → ____

2. ④ → SHAPE → ____ → SHADING → ____ → SIZE → ____

3. 1 → SHAPE → ____ → SIZE → ____ → SHAPE → ____

4. ⑥ → SHADING → ____ → SIZE → ____ → SHADING → ____

5. 3 → SHADING → ____ → SIZE → ____ → SHAPE → ____

6. 7 → SHADING → ____ → SHAPE → ____ → SIZE → ____

7. 5 → SIZE → ____ → SHAPE → ____ → SHADING → ____

8. 1 → SHAPE → ____ → SHADING → ____ → SHAPE → ____

9. ⑧ → SHADING → ____ → SHAPE → ____ → SHADING → ____

10. ② → SIZE → ____ → SHAPE → ____ → SIZE → ____

CHANGING ATTRIBUTES (II)

◆

Begin with one of the figures below. Then change the attributes
one at a time, in sequence.

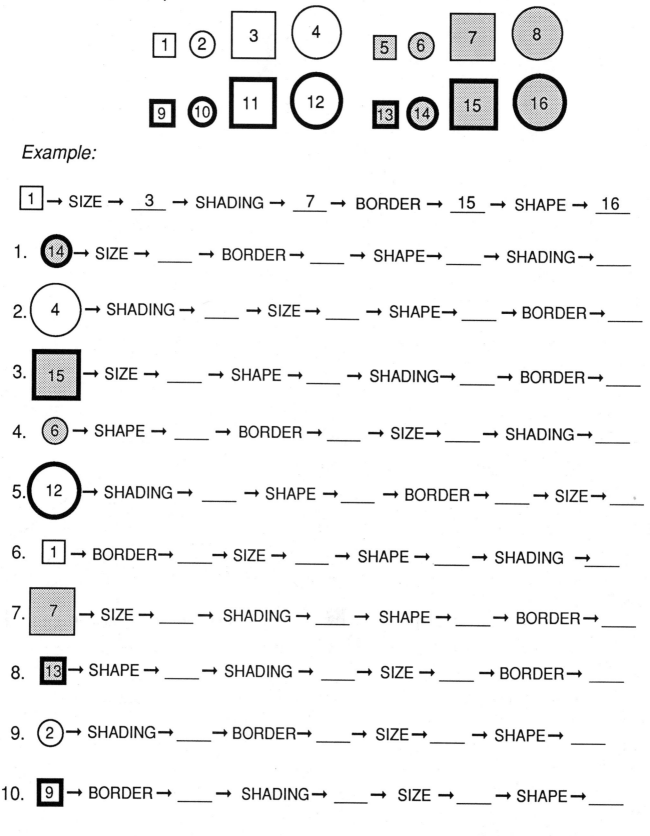

Example:

1 → SIZE → __3__ → SHADING → __7__ → BORDER → __15__ → SHAPE → __16__

1. 14 → SIZE → ____ → BORDER → ____ → SHAPE → ____ → SHADING → ____

2. 4 → SHADING → ____ → SIZE → ____ → SHAPE → ____ → BORDER → ____

3. 15 → SIZE → ____ → SHAPE → ____ → SHADING → ____ → BORDER → ____

4. 6 → SHAPE → ____ → BORDER → ____ → SIZE → ____ → SHADING → ____

5. 12 → SHADING → ____ → SHAPE → ____ → BORDER → ____ → SIZE → ____

6. 1 → BORDER → ____ → SIZE → ____ → SHAPE → ____ → SHADING → ____

7. 7 → SIZE → ____ → SHADING → ____ → SHAPE → ____ → BORDER → ____

8. 13 → SHAPE → ____ → SHADING → ____ → SIZE → ____ → BORDER → ____

9. 2 → SHADING → ____ → BORDER → ____ → SIZE → ____ → SHAPE → ____

10. 9 → BORDER → ____ → SHADING → ____ → SIZE → ____ → SHAPE → ____

CRITICAL THINKING ACTIVITIES IN PATTERNS, IMAGERY, LOGIC (Secondary)
© Dale Seymour Publications

POSSIBLE CONCLUSIONS (I)

For each set of assumptions below, mark each conclusion that will satisfy both assumptions.

Choose:

P = *Possible*

I = *Impossible*

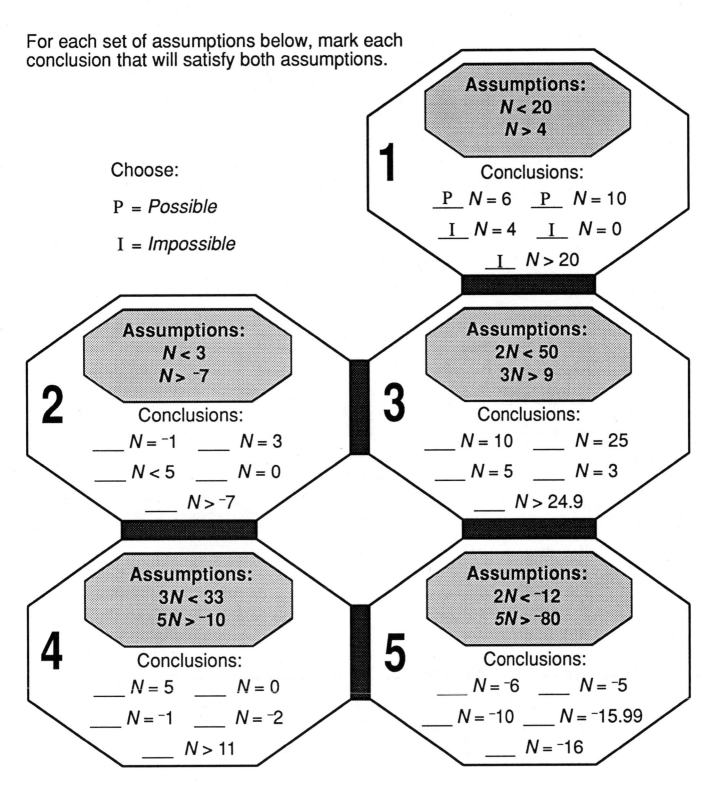

1

Assumptions:
$N < 20$
$N > 4$

Conclusions:

__P__ $N = 6$ __P__ $N = 10$

__I__ $N = 4$ __I__ $N = 0$

__I__ $N > 20$

2

Assumptions:
$N < 3$
$N > {}^-7$

Conclusions:

___ $N = {}^-1$ ___ $N = 3$

___ $N < 5$ ___ $N = 0$

___ $N > {}^-7$

3

Assumptions:
$2N < 50$
$3N > 9$

Conclusions:

___ $N = 10$ ___ $N = 25$

___ $N = 5$ ___ $N = 3$

___ $N > 24.9$

4

Assumptions:
$3N < 33$
$5N > {}^-10$

Conclusions:

___ $N = 5$ ___ $N = 0$

___ $N = {}^-1$ ___ $N = {}^-2$

___ $N > 11$

5

Assumptions:
$2N < {}^-12$
$5N > {}^-80$

Conclusions:

___ $N = {}^-6$ ___ $N = {}^-5$

___ $N = {}^-10$ ___ $N = {}^-15.99$

___ $N = {}^-16$

CHOOSE THE REGION

◆◆

Write the letter of the region where each whole number belongs.

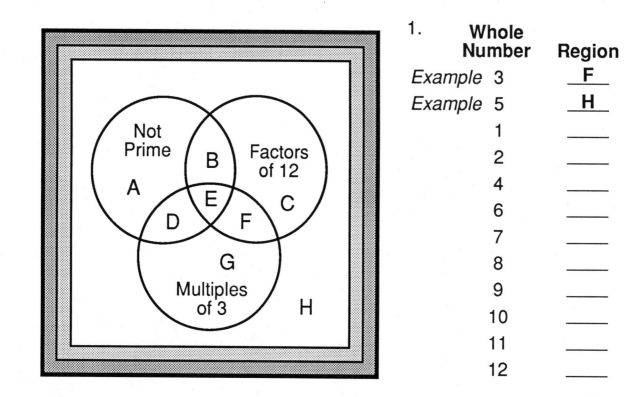

1.

Whole Number	Region
Example 3	**F**
Example 5	**H**
1	___
2	___
4	___
6	___
7	___
8	___
9	___
10	___
11	___
12	___

2.

Whole Number	Region
1	___
2	___
3	___
4	___
5	___
6	___
7	___
8	___
9	___
16	___
18	___
25	___

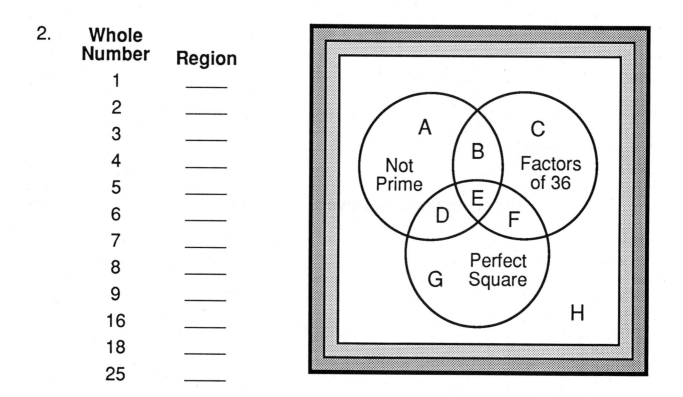

CRITICAL THINKING ACTIVITIES IN PATTERNS, IMAGERY, LOGIC (Secondary)
© Dale Seymour Publications

MYSTERY NUMBERS

Read all of the statements in each problem to determine
whether the conclusion is true or false.

1	My number and your number are both divisible by 8. Therefore, the sum of our numbers will be divisible by 4.	true false
2	My number is equal to Don's number. Don's number is greater than Donna's number. Your number is less than Donna's number. Therefore, my number is greater than yours.	true false
3	My number has two odd repeating digits. My number's digits add up to less than 10. Therefore, my number must be 33.	true false
4	My number is divisible by 5. Your number is divisible by 3. Therefore, our numbers can't be the same.	true false
5	Tim's number is equal to Scott's. Karen's number is greater than Scott's. Todd's number is less than Tim's. Therefore, Karen's number is greater than Todd's.	true false
6	My number is greater than 15. Your number is less than 20. My number is less than 19. Your number is greater than 13. Therefore, our numbers could be the same.	true false
7	Judy's number is greater than Mario's. Dave's number is less than Jeff's. Jeff's number is equal to Mario's. Judy's number is greater than Dave's. Therefore, Dave's number is greater than Jeff's.	true false
8	My number is a whole number. My number is the square root of your number. Your number is less than four times mine. Therefore, your number is a two-digit number.	true false
9	My number is three more than twice Kum's number. Therefore, three less than half my number is Kum's.	true false

NUMBER JUGGLING (II)

◆◆

Use any three of the four numbers 2, 4, 8, and 10 to make the number sentences true. Use each number only once in a problem.

1. $\bigcirc + \bigcirc - \bigcirc = 6$

2. $\bigcirc \times \bigcirc - \bigcirc = 12$

3. $\bigcirc \times \bigcirc + \bigcirc = 34$

4. $\bigcirc \times \bigcirc - \bigcirc = 22$

5. $\bigcirc \div \bigcirc + \bigcirc = 13$

6. $\bigcirc \div \bigcirc + \bigcirc = 12$

7. $\bigcirc \times \bigcirc \times \bigcirc = 64$

8. $\bigcirc \times \bigcirc \div \bigcirc = 5$

9. $\bigcirc \times \bigcirc \div \bigcirc = 16$

10. $\bigcirc \times \bigcirc \div \bigcirc = 4$

11. $\bigcirc \div \bigcirc - \bigcirc = 1$

12. $\bigcirc \times \bigcirc \div \bigcirc = 40$

CRITICAL THINKING ACTIVITIES IN PATTERNS, IMAGERY, LOGIC (Secondary)
© Dale Seymour Publications

JEEBS AND SEMS

◆◆

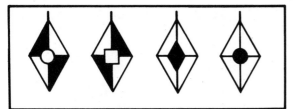 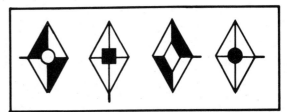

These are all Jeebs.   These are not Jeebs.

1. Which of the following are Jeebs? Draw a ring around each
   correct letter.

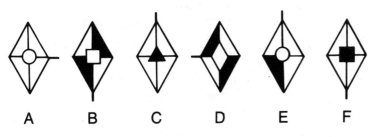

   A   B   C   D   E   F

2. What is the distinguishing characteristic of a Jeeb? _____

_____

These are Sems.   These are not Sems.

3. Which of the following are Sems? Draw a ring around each
   correct letter.

  A   B   C   D   E   F   G   H

4. What is the distinguishing feature of a Sem? _____

DEDUCTIVE LOGIC (I)

◆◆

Six friends each took a turn weighing themselves on the same scale. None of the six weighed exactly the same. The weights were 77 pounds, 81 pounds, 83 pounds, 88 pounds, 95 pounds, and 110 pounds. Use the information given to determine the weight of each person. Mark an X in a space when you have eliminated it as a possibility. Mark an O in the space to show that person's weight.

1. Dianne weighs more than 88 pounds.
2. Barb weighs less than Abe.
3. Faye weighs less than 85 pounds.
4. Carla weighs more than Abe or Faye.
5. Elmer weighs the least of all.
6. Faye weighs more than Barb.
7. Dianne weighs less than Carla.

	77 pounds	81 pounds	83 pounds	88 pounds	95 pounds	110 pounds
Abe						
Barb						
Carla						
Dianne						
Elmer						
Faye						

CRITICAL THINKING ACTIVITIES IN PATTERNS, IMAGERY, LOGIC (Secondary)
© Dale Seymour Publications

CONSTRUCT ATTRIBUTE SETS

Draw all figures in an attribute set with the given conditions.

Example: two shapes: ☐ ◯

two shades: shaded, unshaded

total number of figures __4__

[☐ ◯ ▣ ⬤]

1. two shapes: ☐ △

   two sizes: small, large

   total number of figures: ____

2. three shapes: ☐ △ ◯

   two sizes: small, large

   total number of figures: ____

3. two shapes: △ ◯

   two sizes: small, large
   two shades: shaded, unshaded

   total number of figures: ____

4. three shapes: ☐ △ ◯

   two sizes: small, large
   two shades: shaded, unshaded

   total number of figures: ____

5. three shapes: ☐ △ ◯

   two sizes: small, large
   two shades: shaded, unshaded

   two borders: ☐ ◼

   total number of figures: ____

FIND THE MISSING DIGITS (II)

Find the digits that will replace ⋆ and ¢ to make the problem correct.

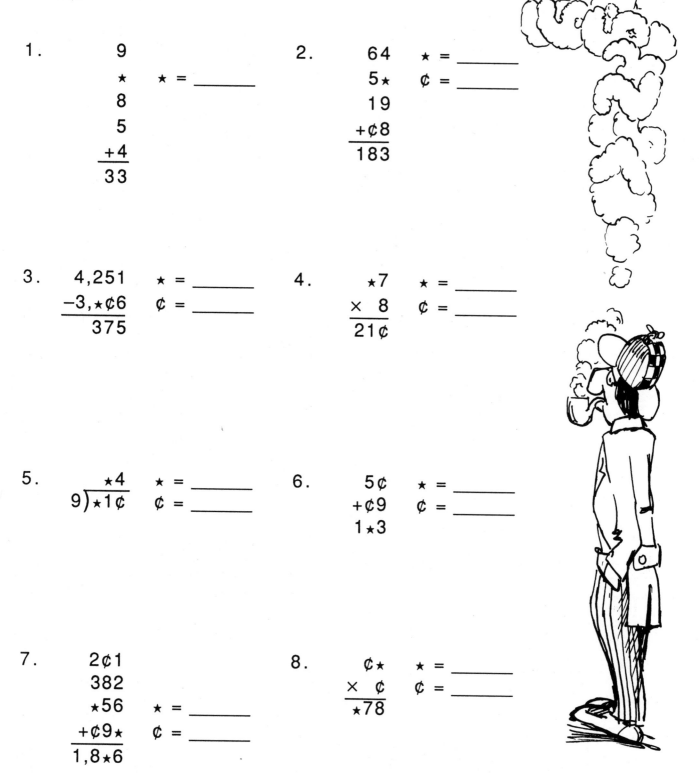

1.
```
      9
      ⋆        ⋆ = _____
      8
      5
    +4
    ────
     33
```

2.
```
     64      ⋆ = _____
     5⋆      ¢ = _____
     19
    +¢8
    ─────
    183
```

3.
```
   4,251     ⋆ = _____
  −3,⋆¢6     ¢ = _____
  ───────
     375
```

4.
```
     ⋆7      ⋆ = _____
   ×  8      ¢ = _____
   ─────
    21¢
```

5.
```
        ⋆4   ⋆ = _____
   9)⋆1¢     ¢ = _____
```

6.
```
     5¢      ⋆ = _____
    +¢9      ¢ = _____
    1⋆3
```

7.
```
    2¢1
    382
    ⋆56      ⋆ = _____
   +¢9⋆      ¢ = _____
   ──────
   1,8⋆6
```

8.
```
     ¢⋆      ⋆ = _____
   ×  ¢      ¢ = _____
   ─────
    ⋆78
```

CRITICAL THINKING ACTIVITIES IN PATTERNS, IMAGERY, LOGIC (Secondary)
© Dale Seymour Publications

COMPARING FACTS TO SOLVE PROBLEMS (II) ◆◆

1. There are five houses in a row. Jack's house is between Alphonso's house and Jane's house. Satomi's house is between Jack's and Jane's houses. Betty's house is between Jack's and Alphonso's. Whose house is the third in the row?

_____

2. Ivan selects a number greater than 10. Sam selects a number less than 6. Cindy's number is greater than 3 but less than 8. Who has the greatest number?

_____

3. Mary is 6 years younger than Ann. Ann is 4 years older than Juan. How does Mary's age compare with Juan's?

_____

4. Ann's weight plus Julian's weight is 230 pounds. Ann's weight plus Allen's weight is 274 pounds. If Ann weighs less than Julian, who weighs the most?

_____

5. Apples cost more per pound than oranges. Grapefruit cost more per pound than oranges but less per pound than apples. Limes cost less than oranges. Pears cost more than grapefruit but less than apples. Which costs more—oranges or pears?

_____

CRACKING CALCULATOR CODES

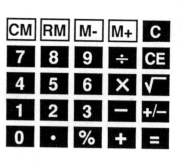

Using this calculator keypad, match the arithmetic problem to the calculator code. After completing the problems, check your work with a calculator similar to the one pictured.

Example: $^-7 \times 4 = ^-28$

Calculator Code: CM C 4 M+ 7 +/− X RM =

Problems: Write in a code letter from below.

_____ 1. $^-4 \times 7 =$ _____ 2. $^-4 + 7 =$

_____ 3. $^-4 - 7 =$ _____ 4. $^-7 + (^-4) =$

_____ 5. $^-4 - (^-7) =$ _____ 6. $4 \times (^-7) =$

_____ 7. $4 + (^-7) =$ _____ 8. $4 - (^-7) =$

_____ 9. $28 \div (^-7) =$ _____ 10. $28 \div (^-4) =$

Calculator Codes: Assume CM and C are pressed before each code.

A. 4 +/− M+ 7 +/− + RM =

B. 4 +/− − 7 =

C. 7 +/− M+ 2 8 ÷ RM =

D. 4 +/− X 7 =

E. 7 +/− M+ 4 + RM =

F. 7 +/− M+ 4 +/− − RM =

G. 4 +/− M+ 2 8 ÷ RM =

H. 4 +/− + 7 =

I. 7 +/− M+ 4 − RM =

J. 7 +/− M+ 4 X RM =

CRITICAL THINKING ACTIVITIES IN PATTERNS, IMAGERY, LOGIC (Secondary)
© Dale Seymour Publications

DESCRIBING ATTRIBUTES

◆◆

The eight geometric figures below illustrate three attributes:
shape (circles and squares), *color* (grey and white), and *size*
(small and large).

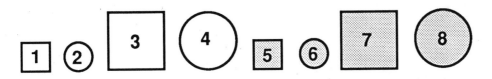

Imagine that all eight figures above are in the rectangle below.
All circles are inside Circle A; all small figures are inside Circle
C. Any large or non-circular shapes are inside the rectangle,
not the circle. Now complete each chart below.

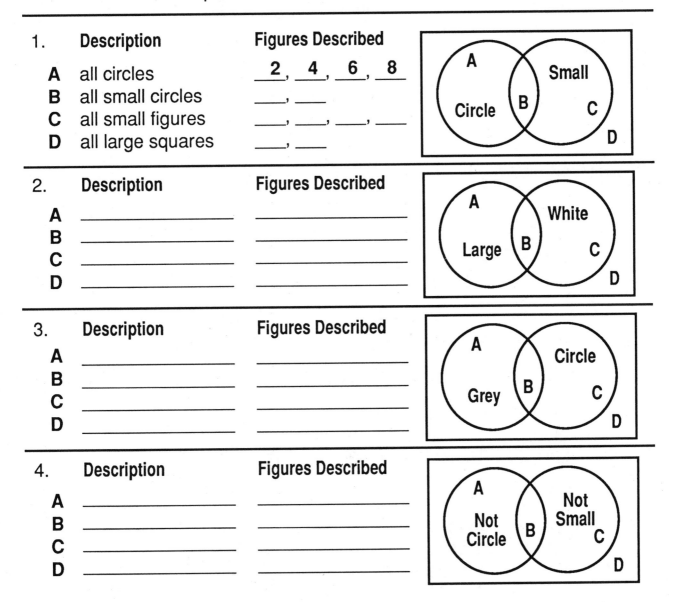

1. | Description | Figures Described |
   |---|---|
   | **A** all circles | 2, 4, 6, 8 |
   | **B** all small circles | ___, ___ |
   | **C** all small figures | ___, ___, ___, ___ |
   | **D** all large squares | ___, ___ |

   Venn diagram: A Circle, Small C, B, D

2. | Description | Figures Described |
   |---|---|
   | **A** ___ | ___ |
   | **B** ___ | ___ |
   | **C** ___ | ___ |
   | **D** ___ | ___ |

   Venn diagram: A Large, White C, B, D

3. | Description | Figures Described |
   |---|---|
   | **A** ___ | ___ |
   | **B** ___ | ___ |
   | **C** ___ | ___ |
   | **D** ___ | ___ |

   Venn diagram: A Grey, Circle C, B, D

4. | Description | Figures Described |
   |---|---|
   | **A** ___ | ___ |
   | **B** ___ | ___ |
   | **C** ___ | ___ |
   | **D** ___ | ___ |

   Venn diagram: A Not Circle, Not Small C, B, D

SOLVING WORD PROBLEMS WITH LOGIC (II) ◆◆

Draw a ring around each correct answer.

1. My number is odd.
   Your number is even.
   Therefore, our numbers differ by 2.   true   false

2. Forty-five is greater than your number.
   Forty-three is less than your number.
   Therefore, your number is less than 48.   true   false

3. Your number is 5 more than my number.
   My number is divisible by 5.
   Therefore, your number is not divisible by 5.   true   false

4. The sum of my number's two digits is 3.
   The sum of your number's two digits is 3.
   Therefore, our numbers must be the same number.   true   false

5. Your number is 3 more than John's number.
   My number is 2 less than John's number.
   Therefore, our numbers are both even.   true   false

6. My number is odd.
   Will's number is odd.
   Therefore, my number is the same as Will's number. true false

7. My number is 2 more than Bob's number.
   Bob's number is 7 more than Zal's number.
   Therfore, Zal's number is 5 less than my number. true   false

8. My number is 2 more than Corazon's number.
   Corazon's number is 5 more than Amy's number.
   Amy's number is 10. Therefore, my number is 17.   true   false

9. My number is greater than A's number.
   B's number is less than my number.
   C's number is equal to A's number.
   Therefore, my number is greater than C's number. true   false

CRITICAL THINKING ACTIVITIES IN PATTERNS, IMAGERY, LOGIC (Secondary)
© Dale Seymour Publications

DECODING WITH LOGIC

◆◆

It's OK to go ahead and solve this problem. But first you need to know that each letter represents a digit and that all O's represent the *same* digit. Here's another clue: O is less than 2, and T is greater than 7. OK, solve the problem!

$$
\begin{array}{r}
OK \\
+TO \\
\hline
GO
\end{array}
$$

What number value (0–9) can be given to these letters to make a correct addition problem? The conditions for the code are given below.

$$
\begin{array}{r}
ADD \\
+FOR \\
\hline
SUM
\end{array}
$$

1. Different letters represent different digits.
2. All three 3-digit numbers are even.
3. The top addend (ADD) is a perfect square.
4. M < D < R
5. D + R > 10
6. O < A < M

MORE DEDUCTIVE LOGIC (I)   ◆◆

This year the officers of the seventh-grade class are Joe,
Allegra, Carmen, and Norma. Use the given statements and
the chart to determine which office each person holds. Mark an
X in a space when you have eliminated it as a possibility. Mark
an O in the space to show that person's office.

1. The secretary is a cousin of Norma's.
2. The president and the treasurer are in the same English class.
3. Carmen is neither treasurer nor president.
4. Joe and the president went to the movies together last week.
5. All five children in the vice-president's family are boys.
6. Norma gets better grades than the president.
7. Joe has one younger sister and one older brother.

	President	Vice-President	Secretary	Treasurer
Joe				
Allegra				
Carmen				
Norma				

CRITICAL THINKING ACTIVITIES IN PATTERNS, IMAGERY, LOGIC (Secondary)
© Dale Seymour Publications

TRUE OR FALSE?

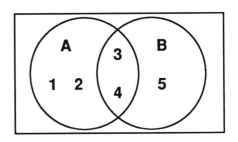

Example: Let A = {1, 2, 3, 4}

         Let B = {3, 4, 5}

  Is 2 ∈ A true?   (yes)

  Is 5 ∈ A true?   (no)

A truth table uses *T* for True and *F* for False.

	$x \in A$	$x \in B$	$x \in A \cap B$
(*x* is 3 or 4) →	T	T	T
(*x* is 1 or 2) →	T	F	F
(*x* is 5) →	F	T	F
(*x* is 6) →	F	F	F

For each pair of sets below, determine which values of *x* satisfy each line of the truth table. Assume the sets are from the whole numbers {1, 2, 3, 4, 5, 6, 7, 8}.

ELEMENTS	$x \in A$	$x \in B$	$x \in A \cap B$
x is ?	T	T	T
x is ?	T	F	F
x is ?	F	T	F
x is ?	F	F	F

Pair of Sets:

1. A = {1, 2, 6, 8}   B = {2, 4, 6}

2. A = {1, 2, 3}   B = {1, 2, 3, 4, 5}

3. A = {M, A, T, H}   B = {P, R, I, M, E}

   Assume the sets are from the alphabet.

PREDICT THE OUTCOME

◆◆

Given a sequence of changes for one of the figures below, try to predict the outcome without working out the steps.

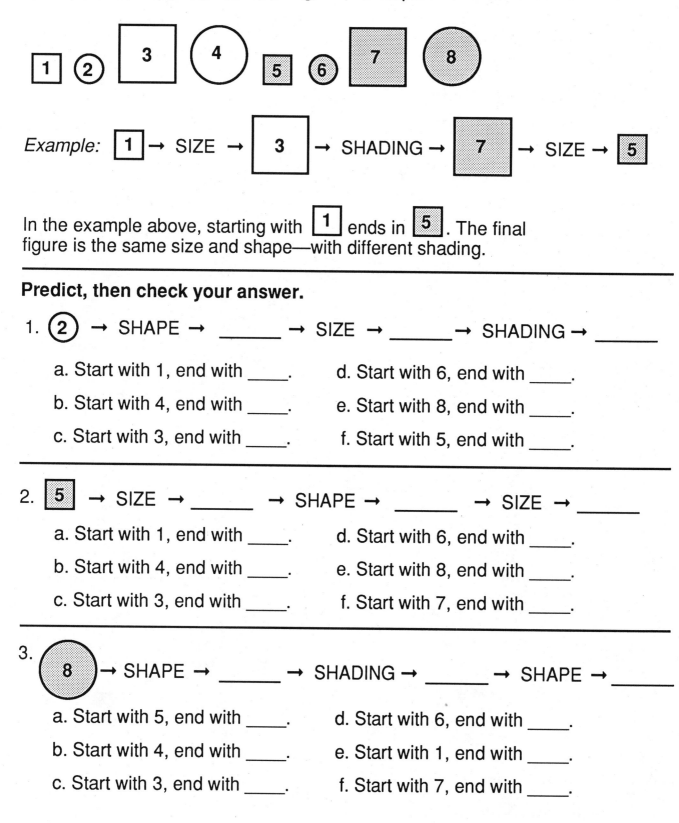

Example: [1] → SIZE → [3] → SHADING → [7] → SIZE → [5]

In the example above, starting with [1] ends in [5]. The final figure is the same size and shape—with different shading.

Predict, then check your answer.

1. ② → SHAPE → _____ → SIZE → _____ → SHADING → _____

   a. Start with 1, end with ____.   d. Start with 6, end with ____.

   b. Start with 4, end with ____.   e. Start with 8, end with ____.

   c. Start with 3, end with ____.   f. Start with 5, end with ____.

---

2. [5] → SIZE → _____ → SHAPE → _____ → SIZE → _____

   a. Start with 1, end with ____.   d. Start with 6, end with ____.

   b. Start with 4, end with ____.   e. Start with 8, end with ____.

   c. Start with 3, end with ____.   f. Start with 7, end with ____.

---

3. ⑧ → SHAPE → _____ → SHADING → _____ → SHAPE → _____

   a. Start with 5, end with ____.   d. Start with 6, end with ____.

   b. Start with 4, end with ____.   e. Start with 1, end with ____.

   c. Start with 3, end with ____.   f. Start with 7, end with ____.

CRITICAL THINKING ACTIVITIES IN PATTERNS, IMAGERY, LOGIC (Secondary)
© Dale Seymour Publications

WINNER'S LOGIC ◆◆

Two people play the game of 5-in-a-row. Taking turns, one
marks X's; the other marks O's. The first player to mark 5 in a
row across, down, or diagonally wins. Answer the questions
below each game. Identify the squares by column letters and
row numbers.

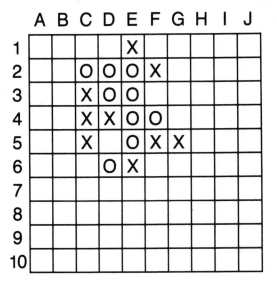

1. It is player X's turn next. What
   square should player X mark?

   _____

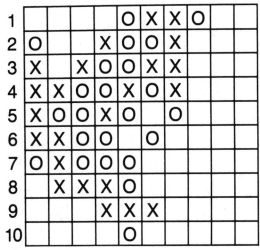

2. It is player O's turn . What square
   will give player O a sure win?

   _____

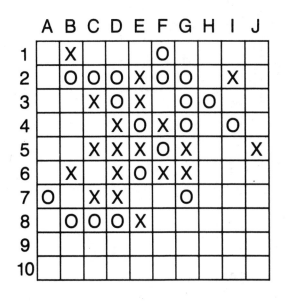

3. It is player X's turn next. What
   square will give player X a sure
   win? _____

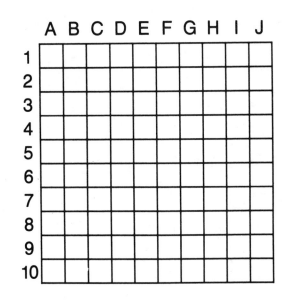

4. Use this grid to play 5-in-a-row
   with a friend.

ADDITION TABLE PUZZLER

◆◆

Here is an addition table in code. Each letter represents a different digit from 0 to 9. The numbers along the top and side are not in any particular order.

Look for patterns that reveal what number each letter represents. Then fill in the letters on the chart below.

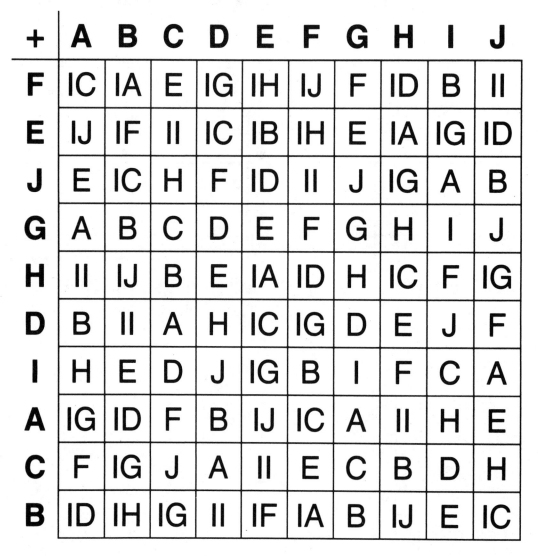

+	A	B	C	D	E	F	G	H	I	J
F	IC	IA	E	IG	IH	IJ	F	ID	B	II
E	IJ	IF	II	IC	IB	IH	E	IA	IG	ID
J	E	IC	H	F	ID	II	J	IG	A	B
G	A	B	C	D	E	F	G	H	I	J
H	II	IJ	B	E	IA	ID	H	IC	F	IG
D	B	II	A	H	IC	IG	D	E	J	F
I	H	E	D	J	IG	B	I	F	C	A
A	IG	ID	F	B	IJ	IC	A	II	H	E
C	F	IG	J	A	II	E	C	B	D	H
B	ID	IH	IG	II	IF	IA	B	IJ	E	IC

Fill in the letters here.

0	1	2	3	4	5	6	7	8	9

CRITICAL THINKING ACTIVITIES IN PATTERNS, IMAGERY, LOGIC (Secondary)
© Dale Seymour Publications

POSSIBLE CONCLUSIONS (II) ◆◆

For each set of assumptions below, mark each conclusion that
will satisfy all three assumptions.

Choose:

P = *Possible*

I = *Impossible*

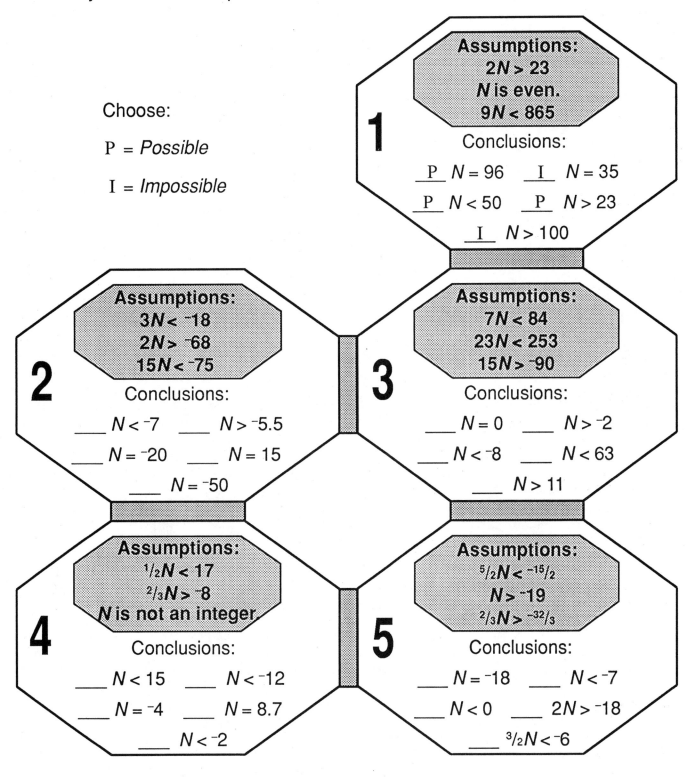

1

Assumptions:
2N > 23
N is even.
9N < 865

Conclusions:

__P__ N = 96   __I__ N = 35

__P__ N < 50   __P__ N > 23

__I__ N > 100

2

Assumptions:
3N < ⁻18
2N > ⁻68
15N < ⁻75

Conclusions:

___ N < ⁻7   ___ N > ⁻5.5

___ N = ⁻20   ___ N = 15

___ N = ⁻50

3

Assumptions:
7N < 84
23N < 253
15N > ⁻90

Conclusions:

___ N = 0   ___ N > ⁻2

___ N < ⁻8   ___ N < 63

___ N > 11

4

Assumptions:
¹/₂N < 17
²/₃N > ⁻8
N is not an integer.

Conclusions:

___ N < 15   ___ N < ⁻12

___ N = ⁻4   ___ N = 8.7

___ N < ⁻2

5

Assumptions:
⁵/₂N < ⁻¹⁵/₂
N > ⁻19
²/₃N > ⁻³²/₃

Conclusions:

___ N = ⁻18   ___ N < ⁻7

___ N < 0   ___ 2N > ⁻18

___ ³/₂N < ⁻6

NUMBER SORT

◆◆◆

Write the counting numbers 1–20 in the appropriate region for each of the three diagrams below.

1.

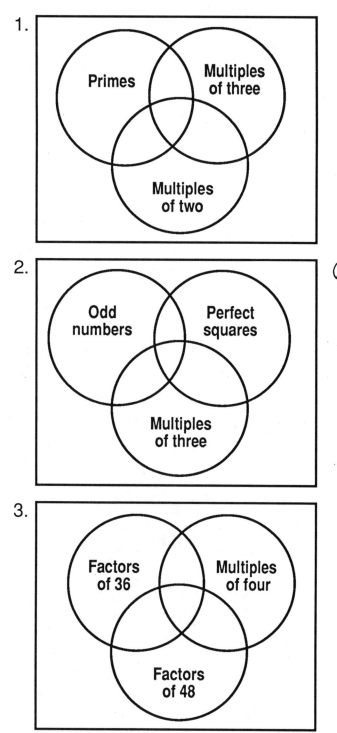

Primes

Multiples of three

Multiples of two

2.

Odd numbers

Perfect squares

Multiples of three

3.

Factors of 36

Multiples of four

Factors of 48

CRITICAL THINKING ACTIVITIES IN PATTERNS, IMAGERY, LOGIC (Secondary)
© Dale Seymour Publications

IT'S UP TO ME!

◆◆◆

IF IT IS TO BE, IT IS UP TO ME.

This sentence is broken up into two addition problems shown at right. Find the values of the letters that will give a correct solution for problem 1 alone, for problem 2 alone, and for problems 1 and 2 together.

1.

```
  IF
  IT
  IS
+ TO
─────
  BE
```

Problem 1 alone:

1. Each letter represents a different digit.
2. All the addends are odd.
3. O > F
4. F > S
5. I > 1

Problem 2 alone:

1. Each letter represents a different digit.
2. All the addends are even.
3. U > T > I
4. P > S > O > T

2.

```
  IT
  IS
  UP
+ TO
─────
  ME
```

Problems 1 and 2 together:

1. The same letters represent the same numbers in both problems.
2. All letters represent different digits except for P and F. P and F represent the same digit.
3. The two letters that look like numbers represent the numbers they resemble.
4. E is a square number.
5. M is a cubed number.

GEOMETRIC CONCLUSIONS

A POLYGON is a closed, plane figure with sides that are line segments.

A QUADRILATERAL is a polygon with four sides.

A PARALLELOGRAM is a quadrilateral with two pairs of parallel sides.

A TRAPEZOID is a quadrilateral with exactly one pair of parallel sides.

A RECTANGLE is a quadrilateral with four right angles.

A SQUARE is a rectangle with four equal sides.

A RHOMBUS is an equilateral quadrilateral.

Complete each sentence below with the appropriate phrase:

can be　　　*is always*　　　*is never*

1. A parallelogram _____ a polygon.	16. A quadrilateral _____ a square.
2. A parallelogram _____ a rectangle.	17. A parallelogram _____ a rhombus.
3. A rectangle _____ a square.	18. A rhombus _____ a quadrilateral.
4. A quadrilateral _____ a rhombus.	19. A rectangle _____ a rhombus.
5. A trapezoid _____ a square.	20. A quadrilateral _____ a trapezoid.
6. A square _____ a rectangle.	21. A trapezoid _____ a parallelogram.
7. A rectangle _____ a parallelogram.	22. A square _____ a trapezoid.
8. A parallelogram _____ a square.	23. A rhombus _____ a rectangle.
9. A quadrilateral _____ a rectangle.	24. A rectangle _____ a trapezoid.
10. A square _____ a parallelogram.	25. A square _____ a rhombus.
11. A trapezoid _____ a rhombus.	26. A parallelogram _____ a trapezoid.
12. A rhombus _____ a parallelogram.	27. A rhombus _____ a trapezoid.
13. A parallelogram _____ a quadrilateral.	28. A trapezoid _____ a quadrilateral.
14. A rhombus _____ a square.	29. A quadrilateral _____ a parallelogram.
15. A trapezoid _____ a rectangle.	30. A polygon _____ a quadrilateral.

CRITICAL THINKING ACTIVITIES IN PATTERNS, IMAGERY, LOGIC (Secondary)

© Dale Seymour Publications

DEDUCTIVE LOGIC (II)

1. Earl has four friends who are good athletes. Their names are Alice, Bob, Clara, and Manny. Their sports are swimming, golfing, running, and wrestling. Use the information given below to match each friend to the correct sport. Mark an X in a space when you have eliminated it as a possibility. Mark an O to show the correct sport for each person.

a. One of the two girls is a swimmer.
b. The wrestler doesn't know Bob.
c. Alice doesn't like the wrestler.
d. Clara knows the swimmer.
e. Bob, Manny, and the runner live on the same street.
f. The girls are best friends.

	Swimming	Golfing	Running	Wrestling
Alice				
Bob				
Clara				
Manny				

2. Five girls named Jean, Jane, Jan, Joan, and Jill play in the orchestra. They play the flute, the clarinet, the saxophone, the drums, and the trumpet. Use the information given below to identify which instrument each girl plays.

a. Jane likes the drummer but doesn't like the flutist.
b. The flute player lives next door to Joan and across the street from Jan.

c. Jill's best friend plays the clarinet.
d. Jean plays the trumpet but would prefer to play the clarinet.
e. Jan doesn't play the sax or drums.
f. Jill isn't speaking to the drummer.

	Flute	Clarinet	Saxophone	Drums	Trumpet
Jean					
Jane					
Jan					
Joan					
Jill					

NUMBER LADDERS

◆◆◆

Change the first number to the last number in the ladders below, using the given number of steps or less.
Follow these rules:

    1. Change only one digit in each step.
    2. The sum of two-digit neighbors is 9 or less.

Example:

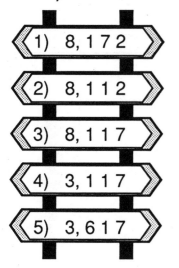

1) 8,172
2) 8,112
3) 8,117
4) 3,117
5) 3,617

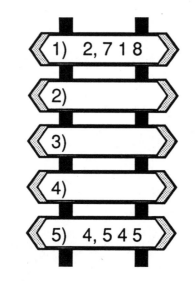

1) 2,718
2)
3)
4)
5) 4,545

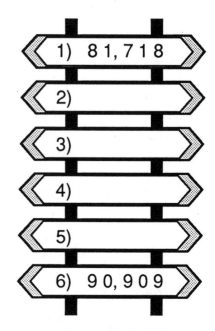

1) 81,718
2)
3)
4)
5)
6) 90,909

For problems 4–6, change rule 2: The product of digit neighbors is an even number.

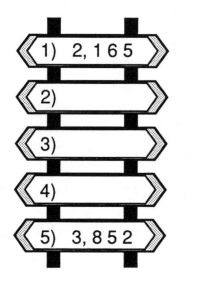

1) 2,165
2)
3)
4)
5) 3,852

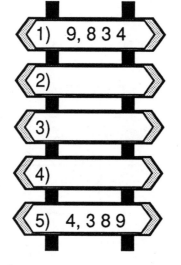

1) 9,834
2)
3)
4)
5) 4,389

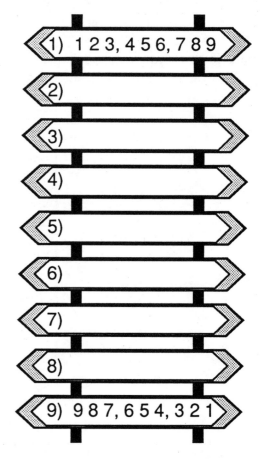

1) 123,456,789
2)
3)
4)
5)
6)
7)
8)
9) 987,654,321

CRITICAL THINKING ACTIVITIES IN PATTERNS, IMAGERY, LOGIC (Secondary)
© Dale Seymour Publications

OUT THINK THE CALCULATORS ◆◆◆

Using this calculator keypad, write the answer that will appear in the display for each code below—and the arithmetic problem for that answer.

Assume **C** and **CM** are pressed before each problem.

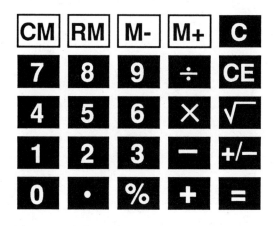

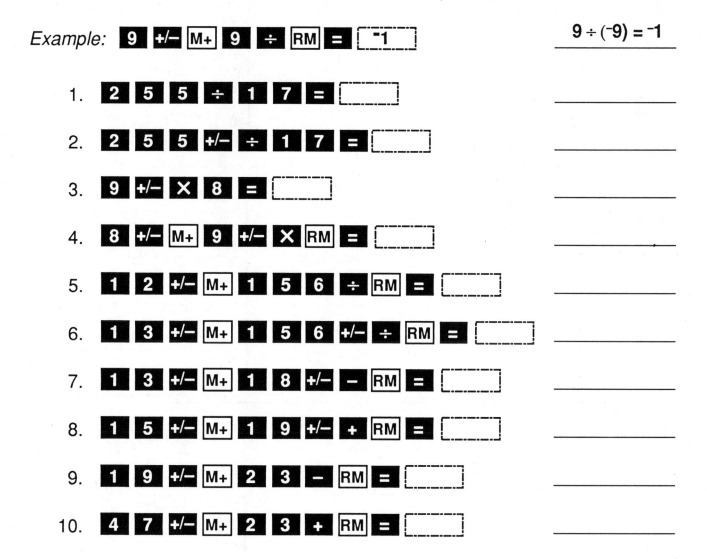

Example: **9** **+/−** **M+** **9** **÷** **RM** **=** ┌ ⁻1 ┐ $9 \div (^-9) = ^-1$

1. **2** **5** **5** **÷** **1** **7** **=** [ ]   _____

2. **2** **5** **5** **+/−** **÷** **1** **7** **=** [ ]   _____

3. **9** **+/−** **×** **8** **=** [ ]   _____

4. **8** **+/−** **M+** **9** **+/−** **×** **RM** **=** [ ]   _____

5. **1** **2** **+/−** **M+** **1** **5** **6** **÷** **RM** **=** [ ]   _____

6. **1** **3** **+/−** **M+** **1** **5** **6** **+/−** **÷** **RM** **=** [ ]   _____

7. **1** **3** **+/−** **M+** **1** **8** **+/−** **−** **RM** **=** [ ]   _____

8. **1** **5** **+/−** **M+** **1** **9** **+/−** **+** **RM** **=** [ ]   _____

9. **1** **9** **+/−** **M+** **2** **3** **−** **RM** **=** [ ]   _____

10. **4** **7** **+/−** **M+** **2** **3** **+** **RM** **=** [ ]   _____

DESCRIBING REGIONS

◆◆◆

The twelve geometric figures below illustrate three attributes:
shape (squares, circles, and triangles), *color* (grey and white),
and *size* (small and large).

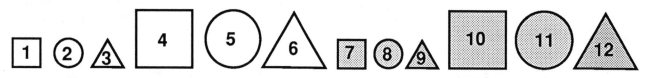

Complete the table for each diagram below.

1.

	Description	Figures Described
A	all circles	2, 5, 8, 11
B	_____	5, 11
C	all large figures	4, 5, 6, 10, 11, 12
D	_____	_____
E	large white circles	_____
F	_____	_____
G	all white figures	_____
H	_____	_____

Circle — B — Large
A — E — C
D — F
White
G — H

2.

	Description	Figures Described
A	_____	_____
B	_____	_____
C	_____	_____
D	_____	_____
E	_____	_____
F	_____	_____
G	_____	_____
H	_____	_____

A — Triangle — B — Small
E — C
D — F
G
Grey — H

3.

	Description	Figures Described
A	_____	_____
B	_____	_____
C	_____	_____
D	_____	_____
E	_____	_____
F	_____	_____
G	_____	_____
H	_____	_____

A — Square — B — Not Small
E — C
D — F
Grey — G
H

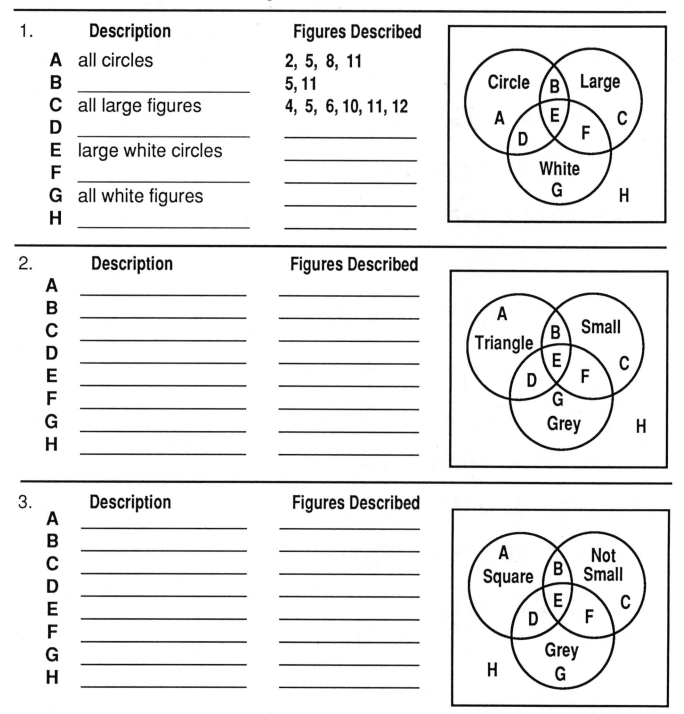

CRITICAL THINKING ACTIVITIES IN PATTERNS, IMAGERY, LOGIC (Secondary)
© Dale Seymour Publications

MULTIPLICATION LOGIC

A, B, and C represent different one-digit numbers. None of the letters represents zero.

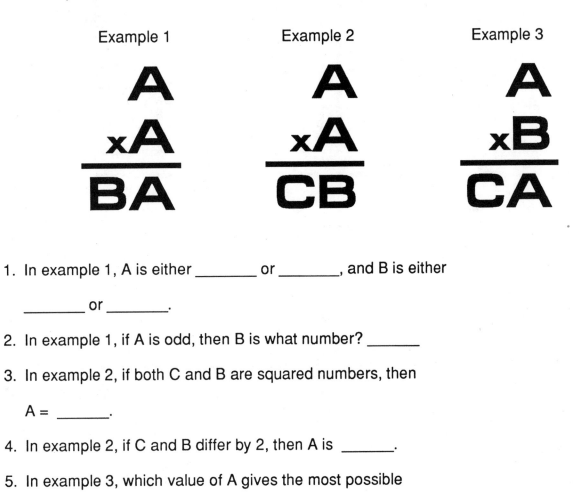

Example 1   Example 2   Example 3

1. In example 1, A is either _____ or _____, and B is either

    _____ or _____.

2. In example 1, if A is odd, then B is what number? _____

3. In example 2, if both C and B are squared numbers, then

    A = _____.

4. In example 2, if C and B differ by 2, then A is _____.

5. In example 3, which value of A gives the most possible

    different solutions? _____

6. In example 3, which value of B gives the most possible

    solutions? _____

CAN YOU GENERALIZE? ◆◆◆

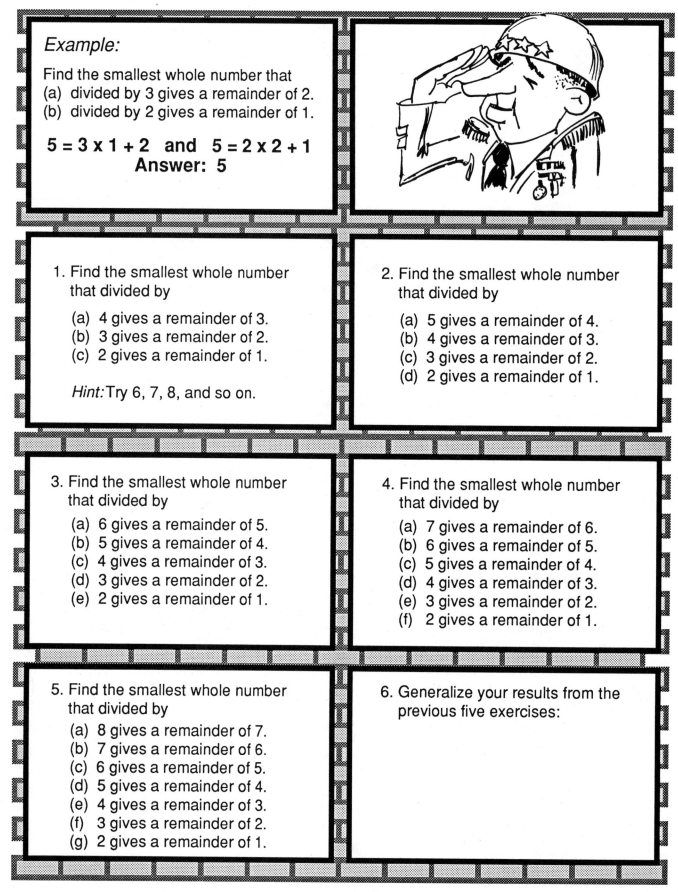

Example:

Find the smallest whole number that
(a) divided by 3 gives a remainder of 2.
(b) divided by 2 gives a remainder of 1.

5 = 3 x 1 + 2   and   5 = 2 x 2 + 1
Answer: 5

---

1. Find the smallest whole number that divided by

    (a) 4 gives a remainder of 3.
    (b) 3 gives a remainder of 2.
    (c) 2 gives a remainder of 1.

    Hint: Try 6, 7, 8, and so on.

2. Find the smallest whole number that divided by

    (a) 5 gives a remainder of 4.
    (b) 4 gives a remainder of 3.
    (c) 3 gives a remainder of 2.
    (d) 2 gives a remainder of 1.

3. Find the smallest whole number that divided by

    (a) 6 gives a remainder of 5.
    (b) 5 gives a remainder of 4.
    (c) 4 gives a remainder of 3.
    (d) 3 gives a remainder of 2.
    (e) 2 gives a remainder of 1.

4. Find the smallest whole number that divided by

    (a) 7 gives a remainder of 6.
    (b) 6 gives a remainder of 5.
    (c) 5 gives a remainder of 4.
    (d) 4 gives a remainder of 3.
    (e) 3 gives a remainder of 2.
    (f) 2 gives a remainder of 1.

5. Find the smallest whole number that divided by

    (a) 8 gives a remainder of 7.
    (b) 7 gives a remainder of 6.
    (c) 6 gives a remainder of 5.
    (d) 5 gives a remainder of 4.
    (e) 4 gives a remainder of 3.
    (f) 3 gives a remainder of 2.
    (g) 2 gives a remainder of 1.

6. Generalize your results from the previous five exercises:

CRITICAL THINKING ACTIVITIES IN PATTERNS, IMAGERY, LOGIC (Secondary)
© Dale Seymour Publications

MORE DEDUCTIVE LOGIC (II)

Hugo Middle School sent nine members of its track team to the conference meet. The nine athletes and the student manager rode in two vehicles, one driven by Mr. Hanks, the track coach, and one driven by Mr. Vadez, a math teacher. Use the information given below to determine which students rode in which vehicle. Mark an X in a space when you have eliminated it as a possibility. Mark an O to show the athlete riding in that driver's vehicle.

1. The pole vaulter, the low hurdler, and the manager are best friends, and they rode together.
2. The shot putter and the sprinter rode in Mr. Hanks' vehicle.
3. The quarter miler and the miler don't get along. They never ride together.
4. The high jumper sat between the long jumper and the sprinter.
5. The quarter miler rode with Mr. Vadez.
6. The quarter miler sat next to the low hurdler.
7. Mr. Vadez's vehicle holds only four passengers.

	Shot putter	Pole vaulter	High jumper	Long jumper	Sprinter	High hurdler	Low hurdler	Miler	Quarter miler	Manager
Mr. Hanks										
Mr. Vadez										

WORD LADDERS

◆◆◆

Transform the word on the top of the ladder to the word
on the bottom by changing only one letter in each step.
Remember: You must form a real word at each step, too.

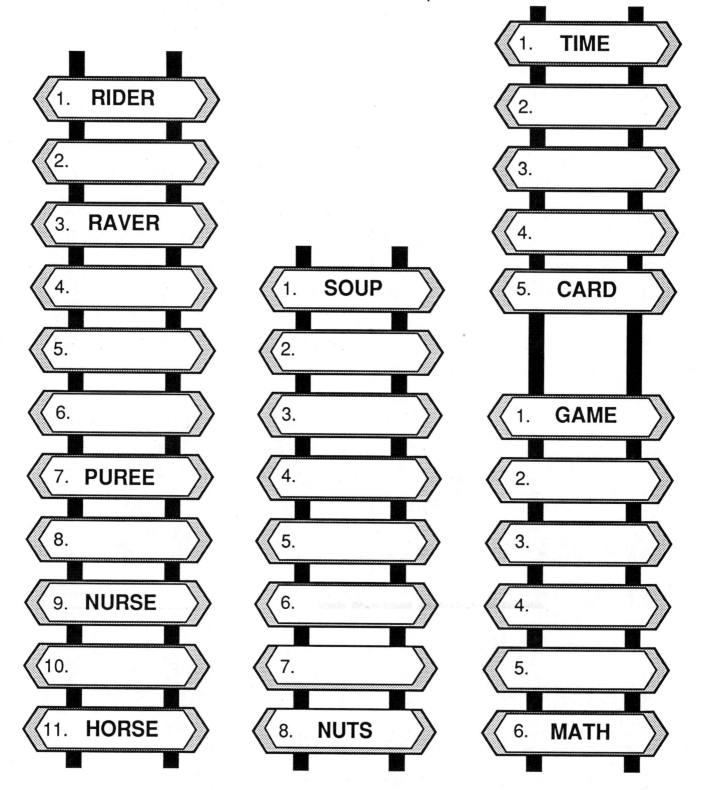

1. RIDER
2.
3. RAVER
4.
5.
6.
7. PUREE
8.
9. NURSE
10.
11. HORSE

1. SOUP
2.
3.
4.
5.
6.
7.
8. NUTS

1. TIME
2.
3.
4.
5. CARD

1. GAME
2.
3.
4.
5.
6. MATH

CRITICAL THINKING ACTIVITIES IN PATTERNS, IMAGERY, LOGIC (Secondary)

BATTLE OF THE CALCULATORS ◆◆◆

Arithmetic Logic

An "arithmetic calculator" with four functions (+, −, x, ÷) computes from left to right as keys are pressed.

Example:

 **6** **+** **3** **×** **8** **−** **4** **÷** **2** **=** `34`

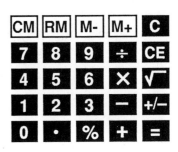

Algebraic Logic

A "scientific calculator" with algebraic logic uses the following order of operations: multiplication (x) and division (÷) first as they occur from left to right; addition (+) and subtraction (−) next as they occur from left to right. The final result is not computed until the "=" is pressed.

Example:

 **6** **+** **3** **×** **8** **−** **4** **÷** **2** **=** `28`

Write the answers using both types of logic below.

Arithmetic   Algebraic

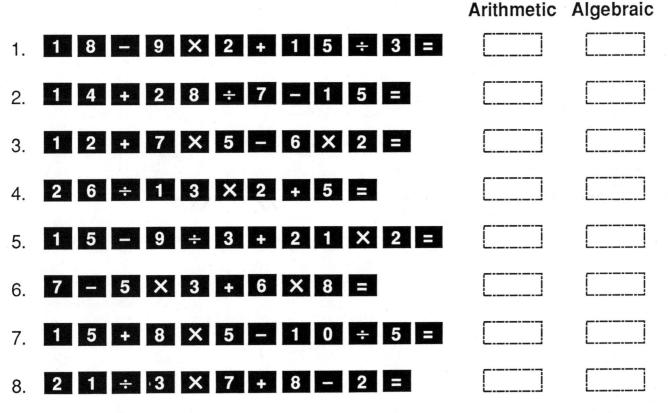

1. **18** **−** **9** **×** **2** **+** **15** **÷** **3** **=**

2. **14** **+** **28** **÷** **7** **−** **15** **=**

3. **12** **+** **7** **×** **5** **−** **6** **×** **2** **=**

4. **26** **÷** **13** **×** **2** **+** **5** **=**

5. **15** **−** **9** **÷** **3** **+** **21** **×** **2** **=**

6. **7** **−** **5** **×** **3** **+** **6** **×** **8** **=**

7. **15** **+** **8** **×** **5** **−** **10** **÷** **5** **=**

8. **21** **÷** **3** **×** **7** **+** **8** **−** **2** **=**

CRITICAL THINKING ACTIVITIES IN PATTERNS, IMAGERY, LOGIC (Secondary)
© Dale Seymour Publications

DIVISION LOGIC

A, B, C, and D each stand for a different one-digit number.
None of the digits is zero.

1. If A = 3 and C = 1, then D = _____ and B = _____.

2. What one-digit numbers can A not be?_____

3. If B is 5 greater than C, then A and D differ by _____.

4. If B is 3 less than C, then D is either _____ or _____.

5. If A is twice D, and B > C, then A = _____, B = _____,

   C = _____, and D = _____.

6. If A + D = B + C, then B = _____ and C = _____.

CRITICAL THINKING ACTIVITIES IN PATTERNS, IMAGERY, LOGIC (Secondary)
© Dale Seymour Publications

WHAT'S THE TRICK?

Work through several examples for each "trick" problem
below. Then explain why the trick works.

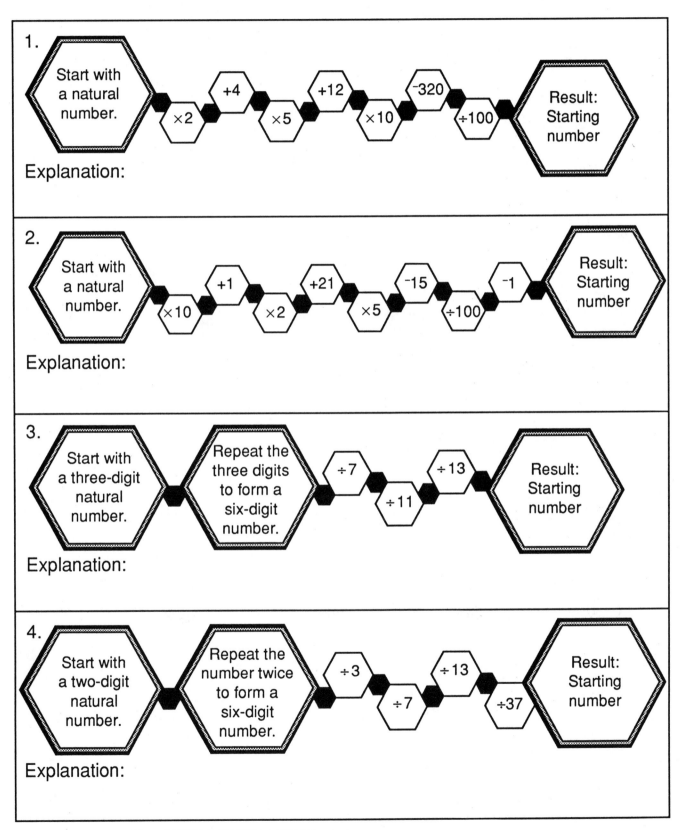

1. Start with a natural number. ×2 +4 ×5 +12 ×10 ⁻320 ÷100 Result: Starting number

Explanation:

2. Start with a natural number. ×10 +1 ×2 +21 ×5 ⁻15 ÷100 ⁻1 Result: Starting number

Explanation:

3. Start with a three-digit natural number. Repeat the three digits to form a six-digit number. ÷7 ÷11 ÷13 Result: Starting number

Explanation:

4. Start with a two-digit natural number. Repeat the number twice to form a six-digit number. ÷3 ÷7 ÷13 ÷37 Result: Starting number

Explanation:

IT'S IN THE CARDS

◆◆◆

Five cards are lying face down. Each pictures an animal. There are one tiger, one emu, one zebra, and two puffins. Using the information given below, identify which card is in each position. Mark an X in a space when you have eliminated it as a possibility. Mark an O to show the position of each card.

1. Neither of the puffins is on either end.

2. The tiger is not next to either puffin.

3. The emu is not in position 2 or 4.

4. The tiger is not in position 5.

5. The zebra is next to the tiger.

	1	2	3	4	5
tiger					
puffin					
puffin					
emu					
zebra					

CRITICAL THINKING ACTIVITIES IN PATTERNS, IMAGERY, LOGIC (Secondary)
© Dale Seymour Publications

JUST FOR FUN

The following are all "Trick Questions."
Each question has a logical answer.
Good luck thinking!

1. How many four-cent postal cards are there in a dozen?

2. How far can you walk into a forest?

3. How much dirt is there in a hole that is three feet wide, four feet long, and two feet deep?

4. There was a blind beggar who had a brother, but this brother had no brothers. What was the relationship between the two?

5. "How much will one cost?" asks a customer. The clerk replies, "Twenty cents." "How much will twelve cost?" The reply, "Forty cents." "I'll take 912." What is the customer buying?

6. Rearrange the letters of NEW DOOR to make one word.

7. If six glasses are arranged in a straight line and the first three are full of water and the last three are empty, what is the fewest number of glasses that can be moved so that the glasses alternate: empty, full, empty...?

8. Horace claimed that "2 × 10 = 2 × 11" is a true statement. What was his explanation?

9. What do all of the following words have in common?

*deft   first   calmness
canopy   laughing   stupid
crabcake   hijack*

10. A train that is one mile long traveling at 60 mph enters a tunnel that is one mile long. How long until the train is out of the tunnel?

11. The distance up a hill and down the other side is the same. A car averages 30 mph going up and 60 mph going down the other side. What is the average speed of the car overall?

12. Write twelve thousand twelve hundred and twelve.

13. Divide 30 by $\frac{1}{2}$ and add 10. What is your answer?

14. What mathematical symbol can be placed between 2 and 3 so that the resulting expression names a number between 2 and 3?

15. A student correctly shows that $\frac{1}{2}$ of 12 is seven. How?

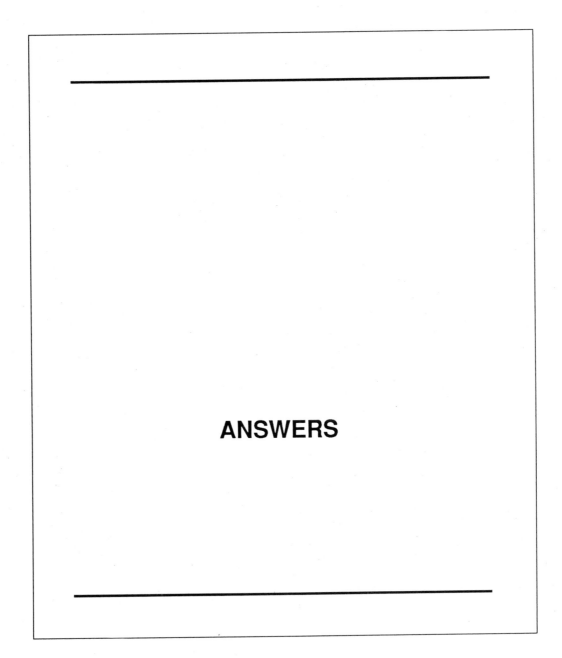

ANSWERS

PART 1: PATTERNS

Page 2, Reversals

1.
```
    962
  − 269
    693
  + 396
   1089
```

2–4. Student work will vary, but results should equal 1,089.

5. Provided students start with a three-digit number in which the digits decrease in value, the reverse-subtract-reverse-add sequence produces 1,089.

6.
```
    9,621
  − 1,269
    8,352
  + 2,538
   10,890
```

7–9. Student work will vary, but results should equal 10,890.

10. Provided students start with a four-digit number in which the digits decrease in value, the reverse-subtract-reverse-add sequence produces 10,890.

11. Yes. Student work will vary, but results should equal 109,890.

12. Six-digit result is 1,098,900.

   Seven-digit result is 10,998,900.

   Eight-digit result is 109,989,000.

Page 3, Patterns of Multiples and Factors (I)

1. 14, 18, 24, 26, 32, 34, 36, 38, 40

2. 2   3. 2, 4, 6, 8, 0   4. 2, 4, 6, 8, 0

5. a, b, d, f, g, h, k, m   6. a, b, c, f, h, j, l

7. a, b, d, e, f, h, k, l   8. True   9. a, c, d, f, h, i

Page 4, Patterns of Multiples and Factors (II)

1. 40, 60, 70, 90, 100, 130, 140, 150, 170, 180, 190

2. 0   3. multiple   4. a, c, e, f, g

5. a. 25, 35, 45, 50

   b. 145, 155, 160, 165, 170

6. 5 or 0   7. c, d, f, g, h, i   8. 5   9. 10

10. a. 12, 21, 24, 27

   b. 117, 123, 126, 129

11. b, c, d, e   12. divisible by 3

Page 5, Patterns of Divisibility

1. a, c   2. a   3. a, e, h

4. a, b, e, f, g, h, i, j, k, l, n, p, q, r

5.
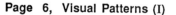

Number	÷ by 2	÷ by 3	÷ by 6	÷ by 9
9		✔		✔
12	✔	✔	✔	
15		✔		
20	✔			
39		✔		
66	✔	✔	✔	

Page 6, Visual Patterns (I)

1.
2.
3.

Page 7, Logic Patterns (I)

1.
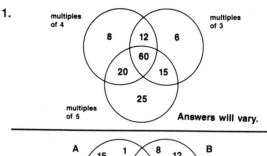

Answers will vary.

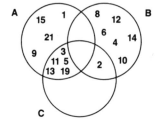

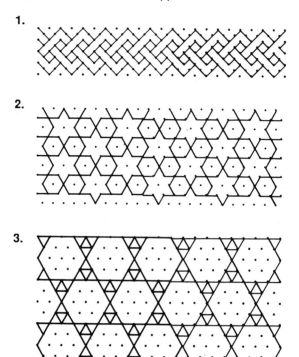

CRITICAL THINKING ACTIVITIES IN PATTERNS, IMAGERY, LOGIC (Secondary)
© Dale Seymour Publications

Page 7, Logic Patterns (I) continued

2. Set A has odd numbers.

3. Set B has even numbers (multiples of 2).

4. Set C has prime numbers.

5. It has odd prime numbers.

6. It has even prime numbers.

7. none   8. none

Page 8, Digit-Sum Average

1. $6\frac{1}{2}$, No   2. 6, Yes   3. $3\frac{1}{2}$, No

4. 5, Yes   5. 5, Yes   6. $\frac{7}{3}$, No   7. 2, Yes

8. 6, Yes   9. $\frac{8}{3}$, No   10. 5, Yes

11. If both digits are odd or both digits are even, then a whole number is produced.

12. If the sum of the digits is divisible by 3, then a whole number is produced.

Page 9, Match the Rule (I)

1. A, C, E

   Answers will vary. For example, the numerators of the answers are not 2.

2. B, D, G

   Answers will vary. For example, B would need to be reordered as $\frac{1}{3}+\frac{2}{3}=\frac{1+2}{3}$ to match the general equation.

3. D. The answers to "Why don't the equations match?" will vary. For example, even if D's fractions are replaced by equivalent fractions with denominator 12, the order would need to be changed to $\frac{4}{12}+\frac{3}{12}=\frac{4+3}{12}$ to get a match.

Note: Students may claim C, F, and G also do not match the general equation. However, if equivalent fractions are used, the equations match the given form.

Page 10, Match the Rule (II)

1. A, B, C, D, F, G, H.
   The general equation is: $\frac{1}{M}+\frac{2}{M}=\frac{3}{M}$

2. B, C, D, E, F, G.
   The general equation is: $\frac{2}{M}+\frac{N}{M}=\frac{2+N}{M}$

Page 11, Kaprekar's Constant

The number 6,174 is called Kaprekar's Constant. It was named after the Russian mathematician who discovered this result in 1955.

Example: 2,916

Start with any four-digit number. (All digits may not be the same.)

Order the digits high to low.   9,621
Then order them low to high and subtract.   − 1,269
   8,352

Repeat the process: High to low   8,532
   Low to high   − 2,358
   Difference   6,174

What did you observe? _____ Kaprekar's Constant (6,174) is generated.

Try 1998:

	High to low	Low to high	Difference
	9,981	−1,899	8,082
	8,820	− 288	8,532
	8,532	−2,358	6,174

Try 7344:

	High to low	Low to high	Difference
	7,443	−3,447	3,996
	9,963	3,699	6,264
	6,642	2,466	4,176
	7,641	1,467	6,174

Try a four-digit number of your own. Describe the results: _____ 6,174 is eventually generated.

Try this variation using the number 3,142:
Reorder only the first and last digits keeping the middle two the same: 3,142
Subtract: − 2,143
   999

Try 2,997:   7,992   5,994
   − 2,997   − 4,995
   4,995   999

Try another four-digit number. Describe your results: 999 is eventually generated.

Page 12, Number Patterns (I)

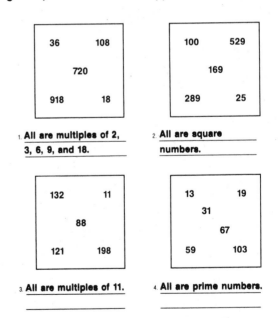

1. All are multiples of 2, 3, 6, 9, and 18.

2. All are square numbers.

3. All are multiples of 11.

4. All are prime numbers.

Answers may vary. These are the most likely answers.

Page 13, Hundreds Chart Patterns (I)

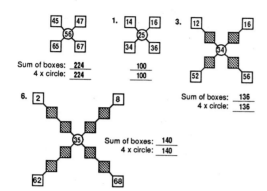

2, 4, 5, 7: Student selections will vary.
Sum of boxes = 4 × circle.

Page 14, Addition Table Patterns (I)

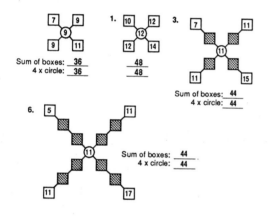

2, 4, 5, 7: Student selections will vary.
Sum of boxes = 4 × circle.

Page 15, Multiplication Table Patterns (I)

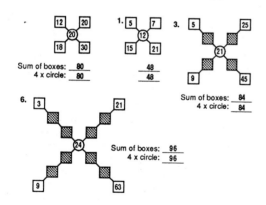

2, 4, 5, 7: Student selections will vary.
Sum of boxes = 4 × circle.

Page 16, Circle Patterns

1–10: Answers will vary.

C + D column should give approximations for π.

Yes. C = π D.

Page 17, Shadow Numbers

Complete each column below. Start with your own number in the last column.				**Answers will vary here.**
Three-digit number	826	471	380	____
Repeat number	826,826	471,471	380,380	____
Divide by 13	63,602	36,267	29,260	____
Divide by 11	5,782	3,297	2,660	____
Divide by 7	826	471	380	____

What number would you multiply 826 by to get 826,826? **1,001**

Four-digit number	3,125	4,605	3,128	____
Repeat number	31,253,125	46,054,605	31,283,128	____
Divide by 73	428,125	630,885	428,536	____
Divide by 137	3,125	4,605	3,128	____

What number would you multiply 3,125 by to get 31,253,125? **10,001**

What is the product of 73 and 137? **10,001**

Two-digit number	23	47	19	____
Repeat twice	232,323	474,747	191,919	____
Divide by 3	77,441	158,249	63,973	____
Divide by 7	11,063	22,607	9,139	____
Divide by 13	851	1,739	703	____
Divide by 37	23	47	19	____

Explain why you get these repeating patterns:

3 × 7 × 13 × 37 = 10,101. Multiplying a two-digit number by 10,101 produces the repeating pattern of the digits.

What is a shadow number?

A shadow number is a number formed by repeating a set of digits at least once. Finding the sequence of divisions to produce the digits is an interesting extension.

Come up with at least one shadow number of your own:

Answers will vary. 444,444 is a shadow number:

Divide by 3 = 148,148
Divide by 7 = 21,164
Divide by 11 = 1,924
Divide by 13 = 148
Divide by 37 = 4

Page 18, Sum Patterns

1. 11   **2.** 11   **3.** 5   **4.** 55   **5.** 50

6. 101   **7.** 101 × 50 = 5,050   **8.** 51 × 25 = 1,275

9. 71 × 35 = 2,485   **10.** 501 × 250 = 125,250

11. $(n + 1) \times \dfrac{n}{2}$

Page 19, Visual Patterns (II)

1.

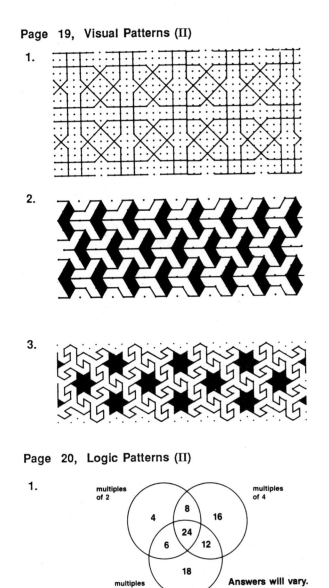

2.

3.

Page 20, Logic Patterns (II)

1.

multiples of 2 — multiples of 4

4, 8, 16, 24, 6, 12, 18, multiples of 6

Answers will vary.

A — B

25, 9, 1, 27, 4, 64, 16, 8, 2, 10, 6, 12, C

2. Set A has square numbers.

3. Set B has cubed numbers.

4. Set C has even numbers.   **5.** 216   **6.** 729

Page 21, Number Patterns with a Rule

	first term $n=1$	second term $n=2$	third term $n=3$	fourth term $n=4$	fifth term $n=5$		rule for nth term	rule for $(n+1)$th term
1.	2	4	6	8	10	···	$2n$	$2(n+1)$
2.	1	3	5	7	9	···	$2n-1$	$2(n+1)-1$
3.	4	5	6	7	8	···	$n+3$	$(n+1)+3$
4.	3	5	7	9	11	···	$2n+1$	$2(n+1)+1$
5.	2	5	8	11	14	···	$3n-1$	$3(n+1)-1$
6.	5	7	9	11	13	···	$2n+3$	$2(n+1)+3$
7.	1	4	9	16	25	···	n^2	$(n+1)^2$
8.	0	3	8	15	24	···	n^2-1	$(n+1)^2-1$
9.	2	8	18	32	50	···	$2n^2$	$2(n+1)^2$
10.	4	7	12	19	28	···	n^2+3	$(n+1)^2+3$
11.	1	8	27	64	125	···	n^3	$(n+1)^3$
12.	1	7	17	31	49	···	$2n^2-1$	$2(n+1)^2-1$

Page 22, Pascal's Triangle (I)

1. Each element is the sum of the two values bordering it in the previous row.

2. 1,716 and 1,716

3. 1, 2, 4, 8, 16, 32, 64, 128, 256, 512...
Row sum = 2^n, where n is the row number.

4. $64 = 2^6$ **5.** $1,024 = 2^{10}$ **6.** 2^{100}

Page 23, Pascal's Triangle (II)

1. Diagonal 1   **2.** Diagonal 2

3. Each row is a power of 11.   **4.** Fifth row

5. Answers will vary.

Page 24, Square Dot Paper Areas

1. Find the area of each set of figures on square dot paper.

	Number of Dots Touched (D)	Number of Dots Within (W)	Area in Square Units (A)	
	3	0	$\frac{1}{2}$	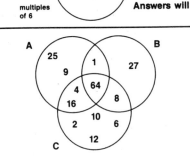
	4	0	1	
	5	0	$1\frac{1}{2}$	
	6	0	2	

2. Use your results from above. Draw a ring around the correct formula below.

$A = D + W$ $A = \frac{D}{2} + W$ $\boxed{A = \frac{D}{2} - 1 + W}$ $A = \frac{D}{2} + 1 + W$

Page 24, Square Dot Paper Areas continued

3. Find the area of each set of figures on square dot paper.

	(D)	(W)	(A)
	3	1	$1\frac{1}{2}$
	4	1	2
	5	1	$2\frac{1}{2}$
	6	1	3

4. Use your results from above. Draw a ring around the correct formula below.

$A = D + W$ $A = \frac{D}{2} + W$ $\boxed{A = \frac{D}{2} - 1 + W}$ $A = \frac{D}{2} + 1 + W$

5. Use square dot paper to draw polygons having two inside dots. What formula will relate A, D, and W?

$A = \frac{D}{2} - 1 + W$

6. Perform the same experiment with three inside dots. What formula will relate A, D, and W?

$A = \frac{D}{2} - 1 + W$

Page 25, Bingo Patterns (I)

1.

B	I	N	G	O
⊠	21	33	60	75
9	⊠	32	48	64
7	18	free	54	69
14	28	42	⊠	70
6	24	48	50	⊠

2.

B	I	N	G	O
6	27	42	(57)	65
14	28	49	(51)	70
9	21	free	(60)	62
8	24	33	(48)	64
3	16	32	(54)	66

Page 26, Number Patterns (II)

1. Each third digit is the sum of the first and second digits.

2. They are all multiples of 9.

3. They are all multiples of 8.

4. They are all cubed numbers.

Answers may vary. These are the most likely answers.

Page 27, Geometric Patterns

1. 6   2. 15   3. 16   4. 25   5. 100

8. second and third   9. third and fourth

10. triangular, third   11. third triangular, fourth square

12. ninth and tenth triangular numbers

13. 99th triangular number and 100th square number

Page 28, Winner Patterns (I)

1. The player with the higher multiple of 3.

2. The player having the largest prime number.

Page 29, Number Patterns (III)

1. Complete and extend each pattern:

Set 1	Set 2
$9 + 9 = 18$	$9 \times 9 = 81$
$24 + 3 = 27$	$24 \times 3 = 72$
$47 + 2 = 49$	$47 \times 2 = 94$
$497 + 2 = 499$	$497 \times 2 = 994$
$4,997 + 2 = 4,999$	$4,997 \times 2 = 9,994$
$49,997 + 2 = 49,999$	$49,997 \times 2 = 99,994$
$499,997 + 2 = 499,999$	$499,997 \times 2 = 999,994$
$4,999,997 + 2 = 4,999,999$	$4,999,997 \times 2 = 9,999,994$

Compare the two sets of patterns. Describe your results:

The answers in the two columns are the reverse of each other.

2. Extend this pattern:

$$1 = (1)^2$$
$$1 + 2 + 1 = (1 + 1)^2$$
$$1 + 2 + 3 + 2 + 1 = (1 + 1 + 1)^2$$
$$1 + 2 + 3 + 4 + 3 + 2 + 1 = (1 + 1 + 1 + 1)^2$$
$$1 + 2 + 3 + 4 + 5 + 4 + 3 + 2 + 1 = (1 + 1 + 1 + 1 + 1)^2$$
$$1 + 2 + 3 + 4 + 5 + 6 + 5 + 4 + 3 + 2 + 1 = (1 + 1 + 1 + 1 + 1 + 1)^2$$

Describe your results: $n^2 = 1 + 2 + \ldots + n - 1 + n + n - 1 + n - 2 + \ldots + 1$

3. Extend this pattern:

$$1 \times 2 \times 3 \times 4 + 1 = 25 = 5^2$$
$$2 \times 3 \times 4 \times 5 + 1 = 121 = 11^2$$
$$3 \times 4 \times 5 \times 6 + 1 = 361 = 19^2$$
$$4 \times 5 \times 6 \times 7 + 1 = 841 = 29^2$$
$$5 \times 6 \times 7 \times 8 + 1 = 1,681 = 41^2$$
$$6 \times 7 \times 8 \times 9 + 1 = 3,025 = 55^2$$

Describe your results:

$n \times (n + 1) \times (n + 2) \times (n + 3) + 1$ produces a perfect square number.

4. Extend this pattern:

$$1^2 + 2^2 + 2^2 = 9 = 3^2$$
$$2^2 + 3^2 + 6^2 = 49 = 7^2$$
$$3^2 + 4^2 + 12^2 = 169 = 13^2$$
$$4^2 + 5^2 + 20^2 = 441 = 21^2$$
$$5^2 + 6^2 + 30^2 = 961 = 31^2$$
$$6^2 + 7^2 + 42^2 = 1,849 = 43^2$$

Describe your results:

$a^2 + b^2 + (ab)^2$ produces a perfect square number.

Page 30, Hundreds Chart Patterns (II)

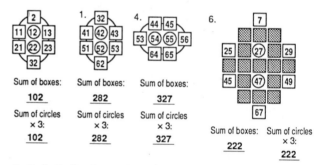

Sum of boxes: **102**   Sum of boxes: **282**   Sum of boxes: **327**

Sum of circles × 3: **102**   Sum of circles × 3: **282**   Sum of circles × 3: **327**

Sum of boxes: **222**   Sum of circles × 3: **222**

2, 3, 5, 7: Student selections will vary.

Sum of boxes = (Sum of circles) × 3

8. Answers will vary.

Page 31, Addition Table Patterns (II)

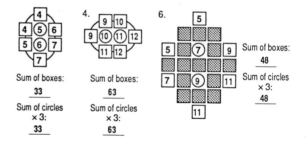

Sum of boxes: **33**   Sum of boxes: **63**   Sum of boxes: **48**

Sum of circles × 3: **33**   Sum of circles × 3: **63**   Sum of circles × 3: **48**

Page 31, Addition Table Patterns (II) continued

1, 2, 3, 5, 7: Student selections will vary.
Sum of boxes = (Sum of circles) × 3

8. Answers will vary.

Page 32, Multiplication Table Patterns (II)

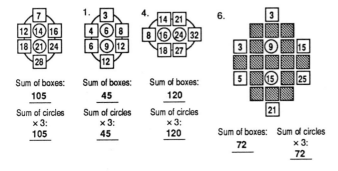

Sum of boxes:
105

Sum of circles × 3:
105

Sum of boxes:
45

Sum of circles × 3:
45

Sum of boxes:
120

Sum of circles × 3:
120

Sum of boxes: **72**   Sum of circles × 3: **72**

2, 3, 5, 7: Student selections will vary.
Sum of boxes = (Sum of circles) × 3

8. Answers will vary.

Page 33, Polyhedron Patterns

Hexahedron: 6, 8, 12, 6 + 8 − 12 = 2

Octahedron: 8, 6, 12, 8 + 6 − 12 = 2

Dodecahedron: 12, 20, 30, 12 + 20 − 30 = 2

Icosahedron: 20, 12, 30, 20 + 12 − 30 = 2

1. F + V − E always equals 2.

2. F + V − E = 6 + 8 − 12 = 2.

3. Student selections will vary. However, for any simple polyhedron, F + V − E = 2 (Euler's Theorem).

Page 34, Odd Integer Patterns

1. 1   **2.** 4   **3.** 9   **4.** 16   **5.** 25   **6.** 36

7. 49   **8.** They are all squares.

9. The sum of consecutive odd integers equals the square of the number of terms.

10. 3   **11.** 4   **12.** 5   **13.** 6   **14.** 7   **15.** 11

16. 16   **17.** 30   **18.** 50

19. Divide the sum of the first and last terms by 2.

20. 625   **21.** 900   **22.** 2,500   **23.** 3,844

24. 8,836   **25.** 40,000

Page 35, Farey Sequences

Step 1

F_5 : $\dfrac{1}{2}$ $\dfrac{1}{3}$ $\dfrac{2}{3}$ $\dfrac{1}{4}$ $\dfrac{2}{4}$ $\dfrac{3}{4}$
$\dfrac{1}{5}$ $\dfrac{2}{5}$ $\dfrac{3}{5}$ $\dfrac{4}{5}$

F_6 : $\dfrac{1}{2}$ $\dfrac{1}{3}$ $\dfrac{2}{3}$ $\dfrac{1}{4}$ $\dfrac{2}{4}$ $\dfrac{3}{4}$ $\dfrac{1}{5}$ $\dfrac{2}{5}$ $\dfrac{3}{5}$
$\dfrac{4}{5}$ $\dfrac{1}{6}$ $\dfrac{2}{6}$ $\dfrac{3}{6}$ $\dfrac{4}{6}$ $\dfrac{5}{6}$

F_7 : $\dfrac{1}{2}$ $\dfrac{1}{3}$ $\dfrac{2}{3}$ $\dfrac{1}{4}$ $\dfrac{2}{4}$ $\dfrac{3}{4}$ $\dfrac{1}{5}$ $\dfrac{2}{5}$ $\dfrac{3}{5}$
$\dfrac{4}{5}$ $\dfrac{1}{6}$ $\dfrac{2}{6}$ $\dfrac{3}{6}$ $\dfrac{4}{6}$ $\dfrac{5}{6}$ $\dfrac{1}{7}$ $\dfrac{2}{7}$ $\dfrac{3}{7}$
$\dfrac{4}{7}$ $\dfrac{5}{7}$ $\dfrac{6}{7}$

Step 2

F_5 : $\dfrac{1}{5}$ $\dfrac{1}{4}$ $\dfrac{1}{3}$ $\dfrac{2}{5}$ $\dfrac{1}{2}$ $\dfrac{3}{5}$
$\dfrac{2}{3}$ $\dfrac{3}{4}$ $\dfrac{4}{5}$

F_6 : $\dfrac{1}{6}$ $\dfrac{1}{5}$ $\dfrac{1}{4}$ $\dfrac{1}{3}$ $\dfrac{2}{5}$ $\dfrac{1}{2}$ $\dfrac{3}{5}$,
$\dfrac{2}{3}$ $\dfrac{3}{4}$ $\dfrac{4}{5}$ $\dfrac{5}{6}$

F_7 : $\dfrac{1}{7}$ $\dfrac{1}{6}$ $\dfrac{1}{5}$ $\dfrac{1}{4}$ $\dfrac{2}{7}$ $\dfrac{1}{3}$ $\dfrac{2}{5}$,
$\dfrac{3}{7}$ $\dfrac{1}{2}$ $\dfrac{4}{7}$ $\dfrac{3}{5}$ $\dfrac{2}{3}$ $\dfrac{5}{7}$
$\dfrac{3}{4}$ $\dfrac{4}{5}$ $\dfrac{5}{6}$ $\dfrac{6}{7}$

Page 36, Patterns in Farey Sequences

Sequence	Fraction	Two Neighbors of the Fraction	Sum of Numerators and Denominators
F_4	$\dfrac{2}{3}$	$\dfrac{1}{2}$, $\dfrac{3}{4}$	$\dfrac{1+3}{2+4} = \dfrac{4}{6} = \dfrac{2}{3}$
F_5	$\dfrac{2}{5}$	$\dfrac{1}{3}$, $\dfrac{1}{2}$	$\dfrac{1+1}{3+2} = \dfrac{2}{5}$
F_5	$\dfrac{2}{3}$	$\dfrac{3}{5}$, $\dfrac{3}{4}$	$\dfrac{3+3}{5+4} = \dfrac{6}{9} = \dfrac{2}{3}$
F_6	$\dfrac{4}{5}$	$\dfrac{3}{4}$, $\dfrac{5}{6}$	$\dfrac{4}{5}$
F_7	$\dfrac{2}{3}$	$\dfrac{3}{5}$, $\dfrac{5}{7}$	$\dfrac{2}{3}$

$$\frac{\text{Sum of neighbors' numerators}}{\text{Sum of neighbors' denominators}} = \text{original fraction}$$

Sequence	Sum of Pairs of Fractions Equidistant from $\frac{1}{2}$
F_4	$\dfrac{1}{3} + \dfrac{2}{3} = 1$, $\dfrac{1}{4} + \dfrac{3}{4} = 1$
F_5	$\dfrac{2}{5} + \dfrac{3}{5} = 1$, $\dfrac{1}{3} + \dfrac{2}{3} = 1$, $\dfrac{1}{4} + \dfrac{3}{4} = 1$, $\dfrac{1}{5} + \dfrac{4}{5} = 1$
F_6	$\dfrac{2}{5} + \dfrac{3}{5} = 1$, $\dfrac{1}{3} + \dfrac{2}{3} = 1$, $\dfrac{1}{4} + \dfrac{3}{4} = 1$, $\dfrac{1}{5} + \dfrac{4}{5} = 1$, $\dfrac{1}{6} + \dfrac{5}{6} = 1$
F_7	$\dfrac{3}{7} + \dfrac{4}{7} = 1$, $\dfrac{2}{5} + \dfrac{3}{5} = 1$, $\dfrac{1}{3} + \dfrac{2}{3} = 1$, $\dfrac{2}{7} + \dfrac{5}{7} = 1$, $\dfrac{1}{4} + \dfrac{3}{4} = 1$, $\dfrac{1}{5} + \dfrac{4}{5} = 1$, $\dfrac{1}{6} + \dfrac{5}{6} = 1$, $\dfrac{1}{7} + \dfrac{6}{7} = 1$

The sum is 1.

Page 37, Division Patterns

1.

Start with two numbers:	0.125 and 0.2		
Divide the second by the first:	0.2 ÷ 0.125	=	1.6
Divide the answer by the number above it:	1.6 ÷ 0.2	=	8
Divide the answer by the number above it:	8 ÷ 1.6	=	5
Divide the answer by the number above it:	5 ÷ 8	=	0.625
Continue the process:	0.625 ÷ 5	=	0.125
	0.125 ÷ 0.625	=	0.2

What do you observe?
The result is the original second number.

Page 37, Division Patterns continued

2.
Try these two decimals: 0.8 and 0.4
Divide the second by the first: $0.4 \div 0.8 = 0.5$
Continue the process as before: $0.5 \div 0.4 = 1.25$
$1.25 \div 0.5 = 2.5$
$2.5 \div 1.25 = 2$
$2 \div 2.5 = 0.8$
$0.8 \div 2 = 0.4$

3. Repeat the procedure with $\frac{1}{2}$ and 3:

$3 \div \frac{1}{2} = 6$
$6 \div 3 = 2$
$2 \div 6 = \frac{1}{3}$
$\frac{1}{3} \div 2 = \frac{1}{6}$
$\frac{1}{6} \div 3 = \frac{1}{2}$
$\frac{1}{2} \div \frac{1}{6} = 3$

4. Repeat the procedure with 0.5 and 3:

$3 \div 0.5 = 6$
$6 \div 3 = 2$
$2 \div 6 = 0.333...$
$0.333... \div 2 = 0.1666...$
$0.1666... \div 0.333... = 0.5$
$0.5 \div 0.166... = 3$

5. If students use a calculator on Problem 4 and use an approximation for any of the repeating decimals (like 0.3333333 for 0.333...), then the answers for problems 3 and 4 may differ.

Page 38, Doodling

1. 1, 3, 6, 10, 15, 21, 55

2. 2, 6, 12, 20, 30, 42, 110

3. $1 + 2 + 3 + 4 + ... + 98 + 99 + 100 = 5,050$

4. $\dfrac{n(n + 1)}{2}$

Page 39, Successive Decreases and Increases

2. 4% decrease **3.** 9% decrease **4.** 12% increase

5. 10% decrease **7.** 12% decrease **8.** 4% decrease

9. 8% increase **10.** 28% decrease **11.** a decrease

12. a decrease

Page 40, Chart and Table Patterns

For problems 1–4, student answers will vary.

Page 41, Difference Patterns

Complete each table. Write the rule and find the difference of successive y values.

Rule: $y = (3x - 2)$

x	y	D_1
1	1	
2	4	3 (4 − 1)
3	7	3 (7 − 4)
4	10	3 (10 − 7)
5	13	3 (13 − 10)

1. Rule: $y = 2x + 3$

x	y	D_1
1	5	
2	7	2
3	9	2
4	11	2
5	13	2

2. Rule: $y = 4x - 1$

x	y	D_1
1	3	
2	7	4
3	11	4
4	15	4
5	19	4

3. Rule: $y = 5x + 2$

x	y	D_1
1	7	
2	12	5
3	17	5
4	22	5
5	27	5

Page 41, Difference Patterns continued

Now find D_1 (difference of y's) and D_2 (difference of D_1) for these quadratic relations:

Rule: $y = x^2 + 1$

x	y	D_1	D_2
1	2		
2	5	3	
3	10	5	2
4	17	7	2
5	26	9	2

4. Rule: $y = 2x^2 + 2$

x	y	D_1	D_2
1	4		
2	10	6	
3	20	10	4
4	34	14	4
5	52	18	4

5. Rule: $y = 3x^2 - 1$

x	y	D_1	D_2
1	2		
2	11	9	
3	26	15	6
4	47	21	6
5	74	27	6

6. Rule: $y = 4x^2 - 3$

x	y	D_1	D_2
1	1		
2	13	12	
3	33	20	8
4	61	28	8
5	97	36	8

Now find D_1, D_2, and D_3.

7. Rule: $y = x^3 + 1$

x	y	D_1	D_2	D_3
1	2			
2	9	7		
3	28	19	12	
4	65	37	18	6
5	126	61	24	6
6	217	91	30	6

8. Rule: $y = 2x^3 - 3$

x	y	D_1	D_2	D_3
1	−1			
2	13	14		
3	51	38	24	
4	125	74	36	12
5	247	122	48	12
6	429	182	60	12

9. constant **10.** constant **11.** third, constant

Page 42, Diagonal Patterns

1. 14 **2.** 20 **3.** 27 **4.** 35 **5.** 54

6. 144 **7.** 4,850 **8.** $\dfrac{n(n - 3)}{2}$

Page 43, Sequence Patterns

1. 21, 28, 36, 45; The nth term is $\dfrac{n(n + 1)}{2}$.

2. 16, 25, 36, 49, 64, 81; The nth term is n^2.

3. 2, 6, 12, 20, 30, 42, 56, 72, 90; The nth term is $n(n + 1)$.

4. 1, 8, 27, 64; The nth term is n^3.

5. 1, 5, 15, 34, 65; The nth term is $\dfrac{n(n^2 + 1)}{2}$.

Page 44, Counting Dot Patterns

1a. 25 **b.** 100 **c.** n^2 **2a.** 42 **b.** 132 **c.** $(n + 1)(n + 2)$

3a. 33 **b.** 73 **c.** $8n - 7$ **4a.** 34 **b.** 89 **c.** $\dfrac{n^2 + 7n + 8}{2}$

Page 45, Bingo Patterns (II)

1. **2.**

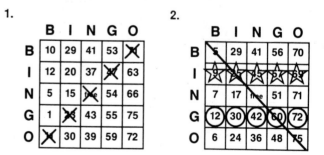

Page 46, Cutting a Cake

2 cuts = 4, 3 cuts = 8, 4 cuts = 15

Additional Activities: b = 5; c = 6

Maximum pieces for five cuts = 26

Page 47, Winner Patterns (II)

1. The player having the lower multiple of 4.

2. The player whose digits total the greater amount.

Page 48, Number Patterns (IV)

1. Extend the pattern:

$$1^2 = 1$$
$$11^2 = 121$$
$$111^2 = 12,321$$
$$1,111^2 = 1,234,321$$
$$11,111^2 = 123,454,321$$
$$111,111^2 = 12,345,654,321$$
$$1,111,111^2 = 1,234,567,654,321$$

When do you think this pattern might not continue?

The pattern continues through $111,111,111^2 = 12,345,678,987,654,321$.

2. Complete the pattern:

$$3^2 + 4^2 = 5^2$$
$$10^2 + 11^2 + 12^2 = 13^2 + \underline{14^2}$$
$$21^2 + 22^2 + 23^2 + \underline{24^2} = \underline{25^2} + \underline{26^2} + 27^2$$

3. Complete the pattern:

$$1^2 - 0^2 = \underline{1}$$
$$2^2 - 1^2 = \underline{3}$$
$$3^2 - \underline{2^2} = \underline{5}$$
$$4^2 - 3^2 = \underline{7}$$

4. Compute each sum:

Pair One: $32^2 + 63^2 + 79^2 = \underline{11,234}$ $23^2 + 36^2 + 97^2 = \underline{11,234}$

Pair Two: $33^2 + 69^2 + 72^2 = \underline{11,034}$ $33^2 + 96^2 + 27^2 = \underline{11,034}$

Pair Three: $39^2 + 62^2 + 73^2 = \underline{10,694}$ $93^2 + 26^2 + 37^2 = \underline{10,694}$

Pair Four: $32^2 + 69^2 + 73^2 = \underline{11,114}$ $23^2 + 96^2 + 37^2 = \underline{11,114}$

Pair Five: $33^2 + 62^2 + 79^2 = \underline{11,174}$ $33^2 + 26^2 + 97^2 = \underline{11,174}$

Page 48, Number Patterns (IV) continued

Compare the sums in each pair. Describe your results.

The sums are equal.

5. Here is another unusual pattern:

$$(88 + 209) \times (88 + 209) = (297)^2 = \underline{88,209}$$
$$(494 + 209) \times (494 + 209) = (\underline{703})^2 = \underline{494,209}$$
$$(998 + 001) \times (998 + 001) = (\underline{999})^2 = \underline{998,001}$$
$$(744 + 1,984) \times (744 + 1,984) = (\underline{2,728})^2 = \underline{7,441,984}$$
$$(494 + 1,729) \times (494 + 1,729) = (\underline{2,223})^2 = \underline{4,941,729}$$

Describe your results.

Answers will vary. The main point is that students note a connection between the repeating terms in the equations and the resulting sums.

Page 49, Patterns Within Patterns

HOW MANY?	Case 1	Case 2	Case 3	Case 4	Case *n* or rule
Diamonds	1 or $\frac{1 \times 2}{2}$	3 or $\frac{2 \times 3}{2}$	6 or $\frac{3 \times 4}{2}$	10 or $\frac{4 \times 5}{2}$	$\frac{n(n+1)}{2}$
Trapezoids	3 or $2^2 - 1$	8 or $3^2 - 1$	15 or $4^2 - 1$	24 or $5^2 - 1$	$(n+1)^2 - 1$
Non-overlapping polygons	4 or $\frac{1(3+5)}{2}$	11 or $\frac{2(6+5)}{2}$	21 or $\frac{3(9+5)}{2}$	34 or $\frac{4(12+5)}{2}$	$\frac{n(3n+5)}{2}$
Vertices	12 or $1(2+9)+1$	27 or $2(4+9)+1$	46 or $3(6+9)+1$	69 or $4(8+9)+1$	$n(2n+9)+1$
Quadrilateral edges *	16 or $\frac{4(3+5)}{2}$	44 or $\frac{8(6+5)}{2}$	84 or $\frac{12(9+5)}{2}$	136 or $\frac{16(12+5)}{2}$	$\frac{4n(3n+5)}{2}$

* Count shared edges twice.

PART 2: IMAGERY

Page 58, Letter Puzzle (I)

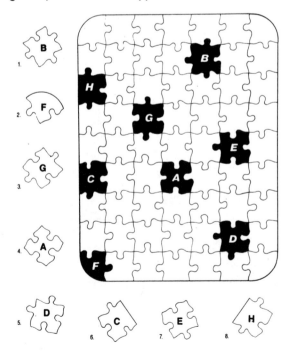

Page 59, Overlapping Figures (I)

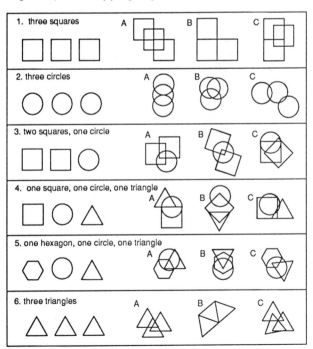

Page 60, Overlapping Figures (II)

The outlines below were produced by overlapping figures. Draw the figures and name them.

Choose from: square, equilateral triangle, circle, rhombus, regular pentagon and regular hexagon.

two figures
square
square

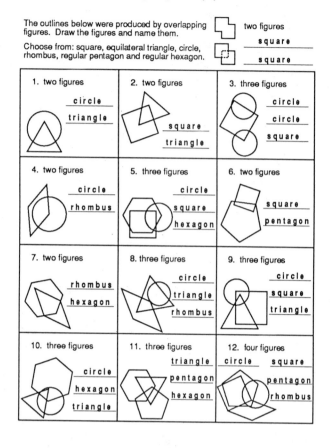

1. two figures	2. two figures	3. three figures
circle triangle	square triangle	circle circle square
4. two figures	5. three figures	6. two figures
circle rhombus	circle square hexagon	square pentagon
7. two figures	8. three figures	9. three figures
rhombus hexagon	circle triangle rhombus	circle square triangle
10. three figures	11. three figures	12. four figures
circle hexagon triangle	triangle pentagon hexagon	circle square pentagon rhombus

Page 61, Direction Codes (I)

1. N–E–S–E   **2.** N–E–S–W–N   **3.** S–E–S–W–N

4. E–S–E–N–W   **5.** E–N–W–S–E–N

6. W–N–W–S–E–N   **7.** South   **8.** North

9. South   **10.** South

Page 62, Direction Codes (II)

1. N–NE–SE–S–E–SW   **2.** S–SW–E–NE–N–SE–E

3. N–E–N–SE–SW–W   **4.** NE–E–SE–S–SW–W–NW–N

5. E–NE–E–SE–SW–N–SW

6. (2) SE   (3) NE   (4) SE   (5) SE

7. East   **8.** North   **9.** Northwest   **10.** South

Page 63, Reflect on These Words

1. Look before you leap.   **2.** All for one, one for all.

3. Absence makes the heart grow fonder.

4. A stitch in time saves nine.

5. Early to bed, early to rise...   **6.** I have a dream...

7. I regret that I have but one life to give to my country.

Page 63, Reflect on These Words continued

8. Smile and the world smiles with you.

9. Big frog in a little pond.

10. Reading backwards is not difficult.

Page 64, Matching Shapes

1. D, E

2. 1–C, 2–B, 3–K, 4–G, 5–F, 6–I, 7–E, 8–A, 9–D, 10–J, 11–H

Page 65, Mirror Images (I)

1. D, F, H, I, J, L   **2.** A, B, G, H, K, L   **3.** A, D

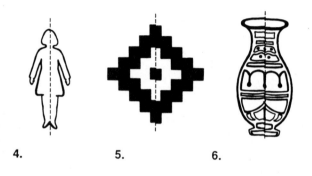

4.   **5.**   **6.**

Page 66, Dot Designs (I)

Page 67, Rotating Gears

1b. CCW **1c.** CW **1d.** CCW

2a. CCW **2b.** CW **2c.** CCW **2e.** CCW **2f.** CW

3a. CW **3b.** CCW **3c.** CCW **3d.** CW **3f.** CW

4a. CCW **4b.** CW **4c.** CW

5a. CCW **5c.** CW **5d.** CCW

Page 68, Stars in Your Eyes

Answers will resemble this figure.

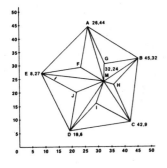

Page 69, Scale Drawings

Drawings will be drawn to scale by students. You might want to make the drawings yourself in order to check students' work.

Page 70, Where Have All the Polygons Gone?

1. 2 **2.** 4 **3.** 2 **4.** 3 **5.** 2 **6.** 8

7. 2 **8.** 4 **9.** 6 **10.** 6 **11.** 6 **12.** 7

Page 71, Map Math

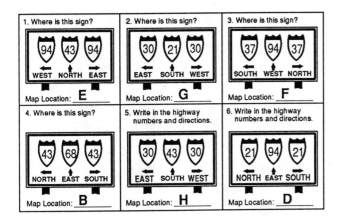

Page 72, Confounding Spiral

Page 73, Letter Puzzle (II)

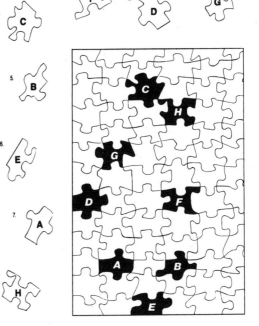

Page 74, Overlapping Panels

Circular panels A–F below are transparent.

A   B   C   D   E   F

The figures in 1–7 were created by overlapping two or more of the six panels. List which of the six panels were used to create the numbered figure.

Example: panels: A, D	1. panels: C, E
2. panels: B, F	3. panels: B, E
4. panels: B, D, F	5. panels: A, B, F
6. panels: C, F	7. panels: A, C, E

Panel X was reflected (flipped) to form Panel Y. The designs below were created by rotating Panels X and Y and placing one over the other, or one over itself. Identify the four pairs of bottom edges in each problem.

X   3   7
Y   6   7

Example: 1 and 5 (and so on)	8. 1 and 1 , 1 and 3 , 3 and 3 , 3 and 1
9. 1 and 5 , 3 and 5 , 1 and 7 , 3 and 7	10. 5 and 6 , 5 and 8 , 7 and 6 , 7 and 8
11. 5 and 5 , 5 and 7 , 7 and 7 , 7 and 5	12. 1 and 6 , 1 and 8 , 3 and 6 , 3 and 8
13. 5 and 4 , 5 and 2 , 7 and 4 , 7 and 2	14. 1 and 4 , 1 and 2 , 3 and 4 , 3 and 2

Page 75, Which Way Subway?

1. F, South   **2.** D, East   **3.** A, North   **4.** E, West

Page 76, Reflect on This

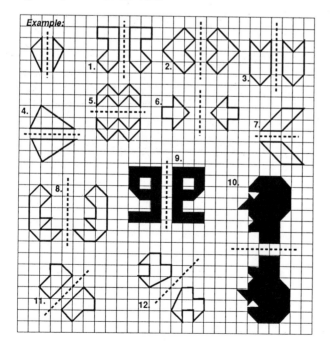

Page 77, Crazy Congruent Shapes

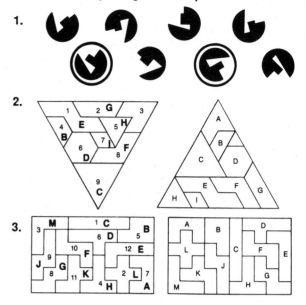

Page 78, Mirror Images (II)

1. A, C, D, F, G, H, J, L   **2.** the Z   **3.** A, B, F

4. A   **5.** D and E

6.

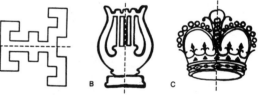

Page 79, Symmetrical Images

Copy each figure on the grid. Does either figure contain symmetry? If so, which one?   **figure 9**

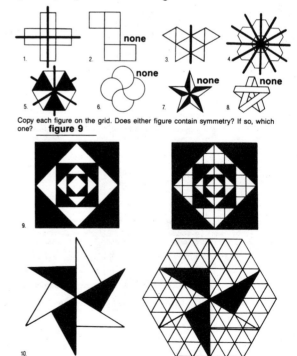

CRITICAL THINKING ACTIVITIES IN PATTERNS, IMAGERY, LOGIC (Secondary)
© Dale Seymour Publications

Page 80, Dot Designs (II)

Copy each design on the blank grid.

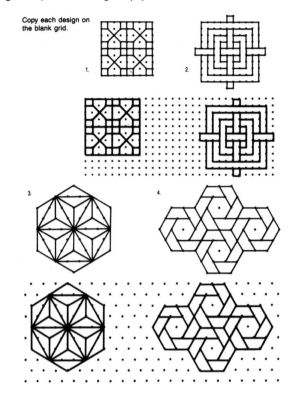

Page 81, Treasure in the Park

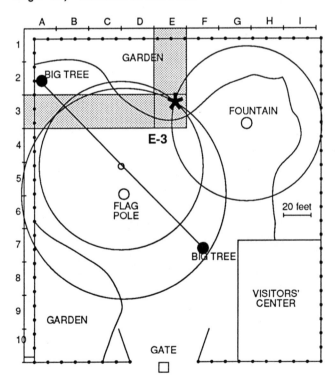

Page 82, Triangle Triumph

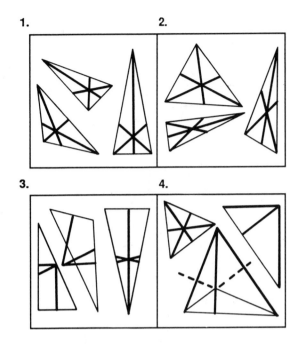

Page 83, Matching Crosses

Page 84, Tangled Triangles

1. 10   **2.** 17   **3.** 16   **4.** 10

Page 85, Map Routes

1. d, e   **2.** b, d   **3.** a, e   **4.** b, c

Page 86, Bar-Rad Ranch

Possible grid locations: F2 and G8

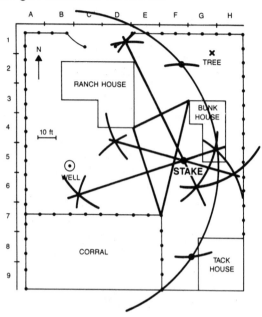

Page 87, Star Locations

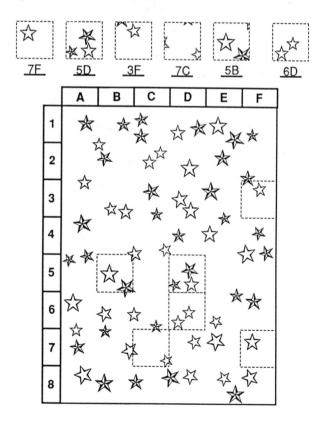

Page 89, Repeater Shapes

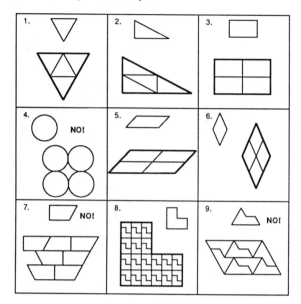

Page 90, Shade Cover

1. B, D, E   **2.** A, C, D   **3.** A, B, F   **4.** B, C, E   **5.** A, B, D

Page 91, Folding Rectangles

1. C, E   **2.** B, F   **3.** A, I   **4.** C, F   **5.** B, F
6. E, G   **7.** E, G   **8.** F, H

Page 92, Divide 'n Congruent

1. The figures that cannot be divided into congruent parts are 5, 7, 12, 21, and 25.

2. 1, 2, 3, 4, 8, 12, 16, 17, 20, 24, 26

3. 1, 8, 9, 19, 20, 24

Page 93, Drawing Mirror Images

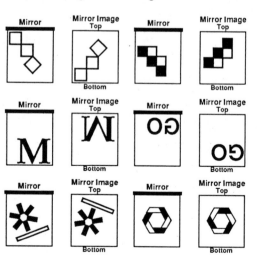

Page 94, Grids and Symmetry

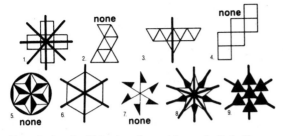

none   none

5. none   7. none

Use a colored pencil or felt-tipped pen. Copy each figure on the blank grids.
Does either figure have a line of symmetry? If so, which one? **neither**

10.

11.

Page 95, It's Your Turn

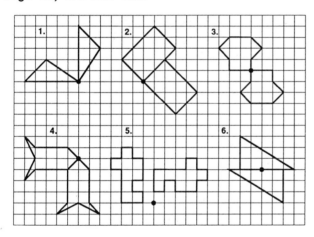

Page 96, Cube Faces

1a. dots **1b.** white **1c.** tiger face

2a. grey **2b.** stars or circles **2c.** diamonds or white

3a. black, white arrow **3b.** black arrow, white

3c. double-black arrow, double-white arrow

3d. double-black arrow, white arrow

3e. white, double-white arrow

Page 97, Find the Shapes

Use these definitions:

Right triangle — a triangle with one right angle.
Equilateral triangle — a triangle with three equal
  sides and three equal angles.
Isosceles triangle — a triangle with two equal sides.

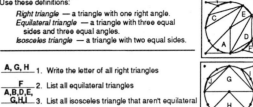

A, G, H 1. Write the letter of all right triangles

F 2. List all equilateral triangles

A,B,D,E, G,H,I 3. List all isosceles triangle that aren't equilateral

C, J 4. List all triangles that are none of the above

By connecting dots with straight line segments:

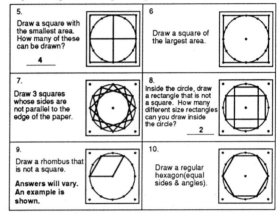

5. Draw a square with the smallest area. How many of these can be drawn? **4**

6. Draw a square of the largest area.

7. Draw 3 squares whose sides are not parallel to the edge of the paper.

8. Inside the circle, draw a rectangle that is not a square. How many different size rectangles can you draw inside the circle? **2**

9. Draw a rhombus that is not a square. **Answers will vary. An example is shown.**

10. Draw a regular hexagon(equal sides & angles).

Page 98, Seeing Stars

Rows: 6A and 6H, 10B and 10G

Columns: 4D and 10D, 4H and 9H

Diagonals: 2F and 4H, 3C and 10J, 2J and 10B

Page 99, Creative Divisions

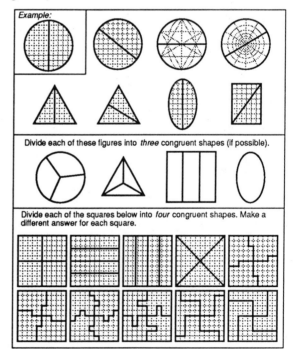

Example:

Divide each of these figures into *three* congruent shapes (if possible).

Divide each of the squares below into *four* congruent shapes. Make a different answer for each square.

Other answers are possible.

Page 100, Match Points

1. D   2. B   3. D

Page 101, Cube View

1. A, B, C   2. A, C   3. B   4. B, D

Page 102, Visualizing Intersections (I)

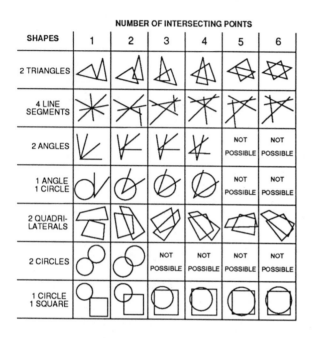

Page 103, Visualizing Intersections (II)

Page 104, Reflected Arrows

Page 105, Tangled Rectangles

1. 9   2. 29   3. 30   4. 94

Page 106, Design Locations

1. 7B, 2B, 6E, 7C, 2C, 4D

Page 107, Fold-a-Form (I)

1. C   2. B   3. C   4. B   5. A
6. C   7. A   8. A

Page 108, Fold-a-Form (II)

1. A, B   2. A, C, D   3. A, B, C, D   4. C, D
5. A, B, D   6. None   7. A, B, C, D   8. B

CRITICAL THINKING ACTIVITIES IN PATTERNS, IMAGERY, LOGIC (Secondary)

Page 114, Figure Sort

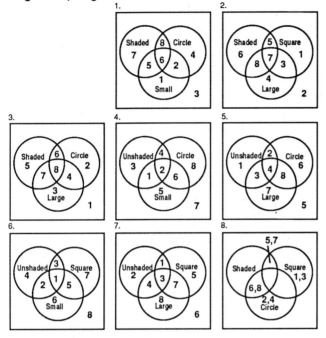

Page 115, Number Juggling (I)

In some cases, the order of these numbers may vary.

1. $12 + 6 + 3$ 2. $12 + 3 - 6$ 3. $6 \times 3 + 2$

4. $12 \times 2 - 6$ 5. $2 \times 3 \times 6$ 6. $6 \times 3 \div 2$

7. $12 \times 3 \div 6$ 8. $12 \div 6 + 3$ 9. $12 \div 2 - 3$

10. $6 \div 2 + 3$ 11. $12 + 2 \div 3$ 12. $6 \times 2 + 3$

Page 116, Logical Families

1. A, C, D, E, F

2. It has two lines connecting the shapes.

3. A, C, F

4. A Setin is a simple shape with the same shape inside it. The outside or inside shape may be shaded.

Page 117, Comparing Facts to Solve Problems (I)

1. Tiffany is shortest.   2. Fred has the least amount.

3. Luis is 6 years older than Jan.   4. 711

Page 118, Inductive Reasoning

1. No   2. Yes   3. Yes   4. No   5. No

6. No   7. No   8. No   9. Yes   10. Yes

11. No   12. Yes   13. No   14. Yes   15. No

Page 119, Number Search

1. 19, 40   2. 14, 19, 24, 29, 40   3. 16, 38

4. 209   5. 18, 25, 31   6. 14, 16, 24, 29, 38

7. 59   8. 9, 12, 15, 17, 18, 22, 25, 30, 31

9. 105   10. 14, 24, 29

Page 120, Find the Missing Digits (I)

1. ★ = 2, ¢ = 8   2. ★ = 7, ¢ = 4   3. ★ = 5, ¢ = 0

4. ★ = 6, ¢ = 8   5. ★ = 9, ¢ = 7   6. ★ = 3, ¢ = 8

7. ★ = 5, ¢ = 7   8. ★ = 4, ¢ = 9

Page 121, Shape Families

1. B, C, G

2. On a Sarm, the shapes on opposite sides of the rectangle are the same.

3. A, B, C, E, G

4. A Lant has three spikes, whereas a Jant has four.

Page 122, Solving Word Problems with Logic (I)

1. True   2. False   3. False   4. True   5. False

6. False   7. True   8. False   9. False

Page 123, Venn Diagrams

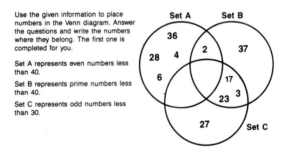

Use the given information to place numbers in the Venn diagram. Answer the questions and write the numbers where they belong. The first one is completed for you.

Set A represents even numbers less than 40.

Set B represents prime numbers less than 40.

Set C represents odd numbers less than 30.

1. 17 is an odd number. It is also a prime number. Therefore it belongs in the part of the diagram that sets B and C share.

2. 36 is a member of set A only.   3. A and B

4. 37 is a member of set B only.   5. A

6. 27 is a member of set C only.

7. 23 belongs to both set B and set C.

8. 6 belongs to set A only.   9. 4

10. None. There are no numbers that are both odd and even.

11. 37   12. 3

Page 124, Addition and Multiplication Logic

A + B = C

1. 6 **2.** 9 **3.** 8 **4.** 9 **5.** 5 **6.** 2

W × X = YZ

1. 7 **2.** 5 **3.** odd, even **4.** W = 4, X = 8, Y = 3, Z = 2 **5.** 5 **6.** Z = 2, Y = 3 or 7

Page 125, Rads, Fads and Hads

1. B, E, F **2.** B, D, E, F **3.** A, C, D, F

4. Answers will vary. It may be a circle, a square, or a triangle having three or four shapes inside it. Of these smaller shapes, two must be triangles.

Page 126, Logical Strategy

1. E8 **2.** F5 **3.** E6

Page 127, Changing Attributes (I)

1. 4, 8, 6 **2.** 3, 7, 5 **3.** 2, 4, 3 **4.** 2, 4, 8
5. 7, 5, 6 **6.** 3, 4, 2 **7.** 7, 8, 4 **8.** 2, 6, 5
9. 4, 3, 7 **10.** 4, 3, 1

Page 128, Changing Attributes (II)

1. 16, 8, 7, 3 **2.** 8, 6, 5, 13 **3.** 13, 14, 10, 2
4. 5, 13, 15, 11 **5.** 16, 15, 7, 5 **6.** 9, 11, 12, 16
7. 5, 1, 2, 10 **8.** 14, 10, 12, 4 **9.** 6, 14, 16, 15
10. 1, 5, 7, 8

Page 129, Possible Conclusions (I)

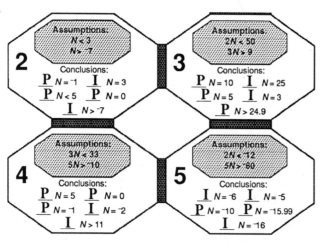

Page 130, Choose the Region

1.	Whole Number	Region
Example	3	F
Example	5	H
	1	B
	2	C
	4	B
	6	E
	7	H
	8	A
	9	D
	10	A
	11	H
	12	E

2.	Whole Number	Region
	1	E
	2	B
	3	C
	4	E
	5	H
	6	B
	7	H
	8	A
	9	E
	16	D
	18	B
	25	D

Page 131, Mystery Numbers

1. True **2.** True **3.** False **4.** False **5.** True
6. True **7.** False **8.** False **9.** False

Page 132, Number Juggling (II)

In some cases, the order of these numbers may vary.

1. $2 + 8 - 4$ **2.** $2 \times 8 - 4$ **3.** $8 \times 4 + 2$
4. $8 \times 4 - 10$ **5.** $10 \div 2 + 8$ **6.** $8 + 4 + 10$
7. $8 \times 4 \times 2$ **8.** $10 \times 2 + 4$ **9.** $8 \times 4 \div 2$
10. $2 \times 8 + 4$ **11.** $10 + 2 - 4$ **12.** $10 \times 8 \div 2$

Page 133, Jeebs and Sems

1. C, E

2. A Jeeb has a spike rising from the top of its diamond shape.

3. A, E, G **4.** It is symmetrical.

Page 134, Deductive Logic (I)

	77 pounds	81 pounds	83 pounds	88 pounds	95 pounds	110 pounds
Abe	✖	✖	✖	O	✖	✖
Barb	✖	O	✖	✖	✖	✖
Carla	✖	✖	✖	✖	✖	O
Dianne	✖	✖	✖	✖	O	✖
Elmer	O	✖	✖	✖	✖	✖
Faye	✖	✖	O	✖	✖	✖

Page 135, Construct Attribute Sets

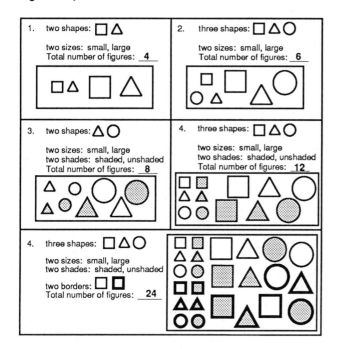

Page 136, Find the Missing Digits (II)

1. ★ = 7   2. ★ = 2, ¢ = 4   3. ★ = 8, ¢ = 7

4. ★ = 2, ¢ = 6   5. ★ = 2, ¢ = 6   6. ★ = 0, ¢ = 4

7. ★ = 7, ¢ = 4   8. ★ = 3, ¢ = 6

Page 137, Comparing Facts to Solve Problems (II)

1. Jack's house   2. Ivan

3. Mary is two years younger than Juan.

4. Alan   5. pears

Page 138, Cracking Calculator Codes

1. D   2. H   3. B   4. A   5. F   6. J

7. E   8. I   9. C   10. G

Page 139, Describing Attributes

1b. 2, 6   1c. 1, 2, 5, 6   1d. 3, 7

2a. all large figures: 3, 4, 7, 8

2b. large white figures: 3, 4

2c. all white figures: 1, 2, 3, 4

2d. small grey figures: 5, 6

3a. all grey figures: 5, 6, 7, 8   3b. grey circles: 6, 8

3c. all circles: 2, 4, 6, 8   3d. white squares: 1, 3

Page 139, Describing Attributes continued

4a. all squares: 1, 3, 5, 7   4b. large squares: 3, 7

4c. all large figures: 3, 4, 7, 8   4d. small circles: 2, 6

Page 140, Solving Word Problems with Logic (II)

1. False   2. True   3. False   4. False   5. False

6. False   7. False   8. True   9. True

Page 141, Decoding with Logic

1. 10 + 81 = 91   2. 144 + 608 = 752

Page 142, More Deductive Logic (I)

	President	Vice-President	Secretary	Treasurer
Joe	✘	✘	O	✘
Allegra	O	✘	✘	✘
Carmen	✘	O	✘	✘
Norma	✘	✘	✘	O

Page 143, True or False?

1. x = 2 or 6   2. x = 1, 2, or 3   3. x = M

x = 1 or 8 x = no values x = A, T, or H

x = 4 x = 4 or 5 x = P, R, I, or E

x = 3, 5, or 7 x = 6, 7, or 8 x = all other letters of the alphabet

Page 144, Predict the Outcome

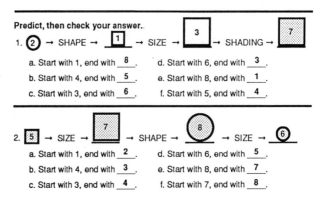

CRITICAL THINKING ACTIVITIES IN PATTERNS, IMAGERY, LOGIC (Secondary)
© Dale Seymour Publications

Page 144, Predict the Outcome continued

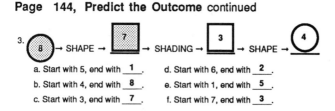

a. Start with 5, end with __1__.   d. Start with 6, end with __2__.
b. Start with 4, end with __8__.   e. Start with 1, end with __5__.
c. Start with 3, end with __7__.   f. Start with 7, end with __3__.

Page 145 Winner's Logic

1. C7   **2.** G7   **3.** C6

Page 146, Addition Table Puzzler

0	1	2	3	4	5	6	7	8	9
G	I	C	D	J	A	H	F	B	E

Page 147, Possible Conclusions (II)

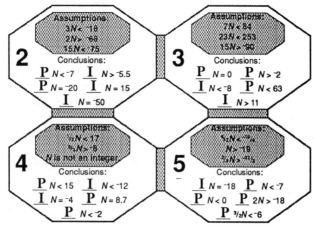

Page 148, Number Sort

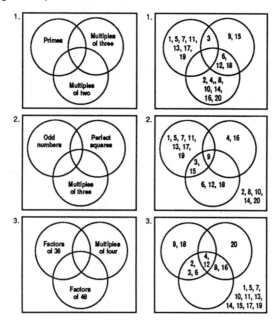

Page 149, It's Up to Me!

Problem 1 alone:
```
  25
  21
  23
+ 17
────
  86
```

Problem 2 alone:
```
  12
  16
  38
+ 24
────
  90
```

Problem 1 and Problem 2 together:
```
  17
  12
  15
+ 20
────
  64
```
```
  12
  15
  37
+ 20
────
  84
```

Page 150, Geometric Conclusions

1. is always   **2.** can be   **3.** can be   **4.** can be

5. is never   **6.** is always   **7.** is always   **8.** can be

9. can be   **10.** is always   **11.** is never   **12.** is always

13. is always   **14.** can be   **15.** is never   **16.** can be

17. can be   **18.** is always   **19.** can be   **20.** can be

21. is never   **22.** is never   **23.** can be   **24.** is never

25. is always   **26.** is never   **27.** is never   **28.** is always

29. can be   **30.** can be

Page 151, Deductive Logic (II)

1. Earl has four friends who are good athletes. Their names are Alice, Bob, Clara, and Manny. Their sports are swimming, golfing, running, and wrestling. Use the information given below to match each friend to the correct sport. Mark an X in a space when you have eliminated it as a possibility. Mark an O to show the correct sport for each person.

a. One of the two girls is a swimmer.
b. The wrestler doesn't know Bob.
c. Alice doesn't like the wrestler.
d. Clara knows the swimmer.
e. Bob, Manny, and the runner live on the same street.
f. The girls are best friends.

	Swimming	Golfing	Running	Wrestling
Alice	O	X	X	X
Bob	X	O	X	X
Clara	X	X	O	X
Manny	X	X	X	O

2. Five girls named Jean, Jane, Jan, Joan, and Jill play in the orchestra. They play the flute, the clarinet, the saxophone, the drums, and the trumpet. Use the information given below to identify which instrument each girl plays.

a. Jane likes the drummer but doesn't like the flutist.
b. The flute player lives next door to Joan and across the street from Jan.
c. Jill's best friend is a sax player.
d. Jean plays the trumpet but would prefer to play the clarinet.
e. Jan doesn't play the sax or drums.
f. Jill isn't speaking to the drummer.

	Flute	Clarinet	Saxophone	Drums	Trumpet
Jean	X	X	X	X	O
Jane	X	X	O	X	X
Jan	X	O	X	X	X
Joan	X	X	X	O	X
Jill	O	X	X	X	X

Page 152, Number Ladders

1. Change only one digit in each step.
2. The sum of two-digit neighbors is 9 or less.

Example:

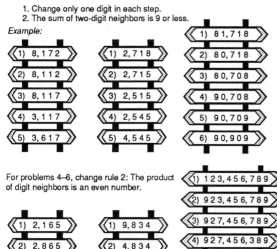

1) 8,172	1) 2,718	1) 81,718
2) 8,112	2) 2,715	2) 80,718
3) 8,117	3) 2,515	3) 80,708
4) 3,117	4) 2,545	4) 90,708
5) 3,617	5) 4,545	5) 90,709
		6) 90,909

For problems 4–6, change rule 2: The product of digit neighbors is an even number.

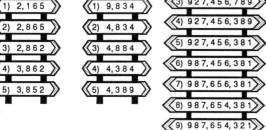

1) 2,165	1) 9,834	1) 123,456,789
2) 2,865	2) 4,834	2) 923,456,789
3) 2,862	3) 4,884	3) 927,456,789
4) 3,862	4) 4,384	4) 927,456,389
5) 3,852	5) 4,389	5) 927,456,381
		6) 987,456,381
		7) 987,656,381
		8) 987,654,381
		9) 987,654,321

Page 153, Out Think the Calculators

1. 15; 255 ÷ 17 = 15
2. ⁻15; ⁻255 ÷ 17 = ⁻15
3. ⁻72; ⁻9 × 8 = ⁻72
4. 72; ⁻9 × (⁻8) = 72
5. ⁻13; 156 ÷ (⁻12) = ⁻13
6. 12; ⁻156 ÷ (⁻13) = 12
7. ⁻5; ⁻18 − (⁻13) = ⁻5
8. ⁻34; ⁻19 + (⁻15) = ⁻34
9. 42; 23 − (⁻19) = 42
10. ⁻24; 23 + (⁻47) = ⁻24

Page 154, Describing Regions

1.

	Description	Figures Described
A	all circles	2, 5, 8, 11
B	large circles	5, 11
C	all large figures	4, 5, 6, 10, 11, 12
D	white circles	2, 5
E	large white circles	5
F	large white figures	4, 5, 6
G	all white figures	1, 2, 3, 4, 5, 6
H	small grey squares and triangles	7, 9

2.

	Description	Figures Described
A	all triangles	3, 6, 9, 12
B	small triangles	3, 9
C	all small figures	1, 2, 3, 7, 8, 9
D	grey triangles	9, 12
E	small grey triangles	9
F	small grey figures	7, 8, 9
G	all grey figures	7, 8, 9, 10, 11, 12
H	large white squares and circles	4, 5

3.

	Description	Figures Described
A	all squares	1, 4, 7, 10
B	large squares	4, 10
C	all large figures	4, 5, 6, 10, 11, 12
D	grey squares	7, 10
E	large grey squares	10
F	large grey figures	10, 11, 12
G	all grey figures	7, 8, 9, 10, 11, 12
H	small white circles and triangles	2, 3

Page 155, Multiplication Logic

1. 5 or 6, 2 or 3
2. 2
3. 7
4. 8
5. 5
6. 6

Page 156, Can You Generalize?

1. 11
2. 59
3. 59
4. 419
5. 839

6. You can get the answer by finding the least common multiple (LCM) of the divisors—then subtracting 1.

Page 157, More Deductive Logic (II)

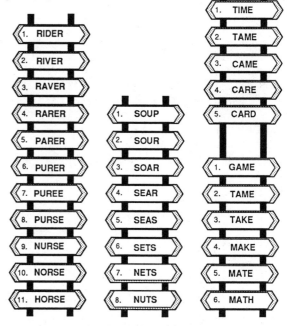

	Shot putter	Pole vaulter	High jumper	Long jumper	Sprinter	High hurdler	Low hurdler	Miler	Quarter miler	Manager
Mr. Hanks	O	✗	O	O	O	O	✗	O	✗	✗
Mr. Vadez	✗	O	✗	✗	✗	✗	O	✗	O	O

Page 158, Word Ladders

| 1. RIDER |
| 2. RIVER |
| 3. RAVER |
| 4. RARER |
| 5. PARER |
| 6. PURER |
| 7. PUREE |
| 8. PURSE |
| 9. NURSE |
| 10. NORSE |
| 11. HORSE |

| 1. SOUP |
| 2. SOUR |
| 3. SOAR |
| 4. SEAR |
| 5. SEAS |
| 6. SETS |
| 7. NETS |
| 8. NUTS |

| 1. TIME |
| 2. TAME |
| 3. CAME |
| 4. CARE |
| 5. CARD |

| 1. GAME |
| 2. TAME |
| 3. TAKE |
| 4. MAKE |
| 5. MATE |
| 6. MATH |

Page 159, Battle of the Calculators

	Arithmetic	Algebraic
1.	11	5
2.	⁻9	3
3.	178	35
4.	9	9
5.	46	54
6.	96	40
7.	21	53
8.	55	55

Page 160, Division Logic

1. D = 7, B = 2   2. 1, 5   3. 1   4. 2 or 7

5. A = 8, B = 3, C = 2, D = 4   6. B = 1, C = 8

Page 161, What's the Trick?

1. Answers will vary. However, the main point is that if students write the "trick" as an algebraic expression, simplifying that expression will yield the starting number.

2. Answers will vary. However, the main point is that if students write the "trick" as an algebraic expression, simplifying that expression will yield the starting number.

3. $7 \times 11 \times 13 = 1{,}001$. Multiplying a three-digit number (such as 567) by 1,001 produces the repeating pattern of the digits (567,567).

4. $3 \times 7 \times 13 \times 37 = 10{,}101$. Multiplying a two-digit number (such as 45) by 10,101 produces the repeating pattern of the digits (454,545).

Page 162, It's in the Cards

	1	2	3	4	5
tiger	O	X	X	X	X
puffin	X	X	O	X	X
puffin	X	X	X	O	X
emu	X	X	X	X	O
zebra	X	O	X	X	X

OR

	1	2	3	4	5
	O	X	X	X	X
	X	X	X	O	X
	X	X	O	X	X
	X	X	X	X	O
	X	O	X	X	X

Page 163, Just for Fun

1. 12.   2. Halfway—then you are leaving the forest.

3. None.   4. Sister.

5. House address numbers at a hardware store.

6. How about ONE WORD?

7. Just one glass. Pour the contents of the middle full glass into the middle empty glass.

8. 2×11 is twenty, too, isn't it?

9. Each word has three letters that appear consecutively in both the alphabet and the word.

10. 2 minutes.   11. 40 mph.

12. 12,000/1,200/12; or 13,212.

13. Would you believe 70?

14. A decimal point (2.3).

15. The Roman numeral for 12 is XII. Draw a horizontal line through this numeral (X̶I̶I̶) and take the top half (VII), which is 7.